_____

NOTARY NAME

_____

COMMISSION NUMBER

Printed Name of Signer	Signer's Signature	Phone No.

Signer's Address

Notary Service(s) Performed ☐ Jurat ☐ Acknowledgment ☐ Oath	Date Notarized	Time ᴬᴹ ᴾᴹ	Fee Charged $
Other Details			

Name/Type of Document	Document Date	Right Thumb Print *(When Applicable)*
Known Personally Y / N ID Type	Issued By	
ID Checked ☐ ID #	Exp. Date	
Notary Service Performed at:		
Witness Name/Address: Witness Signature:		
		Record No.
Notes/Comments:		

Printed Name of Signer	Signer's Signature	Phone No.

Signer's Address

Notary Service(s) Performed ☐ Jurat ☐ Acknowledgment ☐ Oath	Date Notarized	Time ᴬᴹ ᴾᴹ	Fee Charged $
Other Details			

Name/Type of Document	Document Date	Right Thumb Print *(When Applicable)*
Known Personally Y / N ID Type	Issued By	
ID Checked ☐ ID #	Exp. Date	
Notary Service Performed at:		
Witness Name/Address: Witness Signature:		
		Record No.
Notes/Comments:		

Printed Name of Signer	Signer's Signature	Phone No.

Signer's Address

Notary Service(s) Performed ☐ Jurat ☐ Acknowledgment ☐ Oath	Date Notarized	Time AM / PM	Fee Charged $
Other Details			

Name/Type of Document	Document Date	Right Thumb Print *(When Applicable)*
Known Personally Y / N ID Type Issued By		
ID Checked ☐ ID # Exp. Date		
Notary Service Performed at:		
Witness Name/Address: Witness Signature:		
Notes/Comments:		Record No.

Printed Name of Signer	Signer's Signature	Phone No.

Signer's Address

Notary Service(s) Performed ☐ Jurat ☐ Acknowledgment ☐ Oath	Date Notarized	Time AM / PM	Fee Charged $
Other Details			

Name/Type of Document	Document Date	Right Thumb Print *(When Applicable)*
Known Personally Y / N ID Type Issued By		
ID Checked ☐ ID # Exp. Date		
Notary Service Performed at:		
Witness Name/Address: Witness Signature:		
Notes/Comments:		Record No.

Printed Name of Signer	Signer's Signature	Phone No.

Signer's Address

Notary Service(s) Performed ☐ Jurat ☐ Acknowledgment ☐ Oath	Date Notarized	Time AM PM	Fee Charged $
Other Details			

Name/Type of Document	Document Date	Right Thumb Print (When Applicable)
Known Personally Y / N	ID Type	Issued By	
ID Checked ☐	ID #	Exp. Date	
Notary Service Performed at:			
Witness Name/Address:	Witness Signature:	
		Record No.
Notes/Comments:		

Printed Name of Signer	Signer's Signature	Phone No.

Signer's Address

Notary Service(s) Performed ☐ Jurat ☐ Acknowledgment ☐ Oath	Date Notarized	Time AM PM	Fee Charged $
Other Details			

Name/Type of Document	Document Date	Right Thumb Print (When Applicable)
Known Personally Y / N	ID Type	Issued By	
ID Checked ☐	ID #	Exp. Date	
Notary Service Performed at:			
Witness Name/Address:	Witness Signature:	
		Record No.
Notes/Comments:		

Printed Name of Signer	Signer's Signature	Phone No.

Signer's Address

Notary Service(s) Performed ☐ Jurat ☐ Acknowledgment ☐ Oath	Date Notarized	Time AM PM	Fee Charged $
Other Details			

Name/Type of Document	Document Date	Right Thumb Print *(When Applicable)*
Known Personally Y / N ID Type Issued By		
ID Checked ☐ ID # Exp. Date		
Notary Service Performed at:		
Witness Name/Address: Witness Signature:		
Notes/Comments:		Record No.

Printed Name of Signer	Signer's Signature	Phone No.

Signer's Address

Notary Service(s) Performed ☐ Jurat ☐ Acknowledgment ☐ Oath	Date Notarized	Time AM PM	Fee Charged $
Other Details			

Name/Type of Document	Document Date	Right Thumb Print *(When Applicable)*
Known Personally Y / N ID Type Issued By		
ID Checked ☐ ID # Exp. Date		
Notary Service Performed at:		
Witness Name/Address: Witness Signature:		
Notes/Comments:		Record No.

Printed Name of Signer	Signer's Signature	Phone No.

Signer's Address

Notary Service(s) Performed ☐ Jurat ☐ Acknowledgment ☐ Oath	Date Notarized	Time	AM	Fee Charged
Other Details			PM	$

Name/Type of Document	Document Date	Right Thumb Print
		(When Applicable)
Known Personally Y / N	ID Type	Issued By	
ID Checked ☐	ID #	Exp. Date	
Notary Service Performed at:			
Witness Name/Address:	Witness Signature:		
		Record No.	
Notes/Comments:			

Printed Name of Signer	Signer's Signature	Phone No.

Signer's Address

Notary Service(s) Performed ☐ Jurat ☐ Acknowledgment ☐ Oath	Date Notarized	Time	AM	Fee Charged
Other Details			PM	$

Name/Type of Document	Document Date	Right Thumb Print
		(When Applicable)
Known Personally Y / N	ID Type	Issued By	
ID Checked ☐	ID #	Exp. Date	
Notary Service Performed at:			
Witness Name/Address:	Witness Signature:		
		Record No.	
Notes/Comments:			

Printed Name of Signer	Signer's Signature	Phone No.

Signer's Address

Notary Service(s) Performed ☐ Jurat ☐ Acknowledgment ☐ Oath	Date Notarized	Time AM PM	Fee Charged $

Other Details

Name/Type of Document	Document Date	Right Thumb Print
		(When Applicable)

Known Personally Y / N	ID Type	Issued By	

ID Checked ☐	ID #	Exp. Date	

Notary Service Performed at:

Witness Name/Address:	Witness Signature:	
		Record No.

Notes/Comments:

Printed Name of Signer	Signer's Signature	Phone No.

Signer's Address

Notary Service(s) Performed ☐ Jurat ☐ Acknowledgment ☐ Oath	Date Notarized	Time AM PM	Fee Charged $

Other Details

Name/Type of Document	Document Date	Right Thumb Print
		(When Applicable)

Known Personally Y / N	ID Type	Issued By	

ID Checked ☐	ID #	Exp. Date	

Notary Service Performed at:

Witness Name/Address:	Witness Signature:	
		Record No.

Notes/Comments:

Printed Name of Signer	Signer's Signature	Phone No.

Signer's Address

Notary Service(s) Performed ☐ Jurat ☐ Acknowledgment ☐ Oath	Date Notarized	Time ₐₘ PM	Fee Charged $
Other Details			

Name/Type of Document	Document Date	Right Thumb Print (When Applicable)
Known Personally Y / N	ID Type Issued By	
ID Checked ☐	ID # Exp. Date	
Notary Service Performed at:		
Witness Name/Address:	Witness Signature:	
		Record No.
Notes/Comments:		

Printed Name of Signer	Signer's Signature	Phone No.

Signer's Address

Notary Service(s) Performed ☐ Jurat ☐ Acknowledgment ☐ Oath	Date Notarized	Time ₐₘ PM	Fee Charged $
Other Details			

Name/Type of Document	Document Date	Right Thumb Print (When Applicable)
Known Personally Y / N	ID Type Issued By	
ID Checked ☐	ID # Exp. Date	
Notary Service Performed at:		
Witness Name/Address:	Witness Signature:	
		Record No.
Notes/Comments:		

Printed Name of Signer	Signer's Signature	Phone No.

Signer's Address

Notary Service(s) Performed ☐ Jurat ☐ Acknowledgment ☐ Oath	Date Notarized	Time AM PM	Fee Charged $
Other Details			

Name/Type of Document	Document Date	Right Thumb Print (When Applicable)
Known Personally Y / N	ID Type	Issued By	
ID Checked ☐	ID #	Exp. Date	
Notary Service Performed at:		
Witness Name/Address:	Witness Signature:	
		Record No.
Notes/Comments:		

Printed Name of Signer	Signer's Signature	Phone No.

Signer's Address

Notary Service(s) Performed ☐ Jurat ☐ Acknowledgment ☐ Oath	Date Notarized	Time AM PM	Fee Charged $
Other Details			

Name/Type of Document	Document Date	Right Thumb Print (When Applicable)
Known Personally Y / N	ID Type	Issued By	
ID Checked ☐	ID #	Exp. Date	
Notary Service Performed at:		
Witness Name/Address:	Witness Signature:	
		Record No.
Notes/Comments:		

Printed Name of Signer	Signer's Signature	Phone No.

Signer's Address

Notary Service(s) Performed ☐ Jurat ☐ Acknowledgment ☐ Oath	Date Notarized	Time AM PM	Fee Charged $

Other Details

Name/Type of Document	Document Date	Right Thumb Print
Known Personally Y / N	ID Type	Issued By	*(When Applicable)*
ID Checked ☐	ID #	Exp. Date	

Notary Service Performed at:

Witness Name/Address:	Witness Signature:	
Notes/Comments:		Record No.

Printed Name of Signer	Signer's Signature	Phone No.

Signer's Address

Notary Service(s) Performed ☐ Jurat ☐ Acknowledgment ☐ Oath	Date Notarized	Time AM PM	Fee Charged $

Other Details

Name/Type of Document	Document Date	Right Thumb Print
Known Personally Y / N	ID Type	Issued By	*(When Applicable)*
ID Checked ☐	ID #	Exp. Date	

Notary Service Performed at:

Witness Name/Address:	Witness Signature:	
Notes/Comments:		Record No.

Printed Name of Signer	Signer's Signature	Phone No.

Signer's Address

Notary Service(s) Performed ☐ Jurat ☐ Acknowledgment ☐ Oath	Date Notarized	Time AM PM	Fee Charged $
Other Details			

Name/Type of Document	Document Date	Right Thumb Print *(When Applicable)*
Known Personally Y / N	ID Type	Issued By	
ID Checked ☐	ID #	Exp. Date	
Notary Service Performed at:		
Witness Name/Address:	Witness Signature:	
		Record No.
Notes/Comments:		

Printed Name of Signer	Signer's Signature	Phone No.

Signer's Address

Notary Service(s) Performed ☐ Jurat ☐ Acknowledgment ☐ Oath	Date Notarized	Time AM PM	Fee Charged $
Other Details			

Name/Type of Document	Document Date	Right Thumb Print *(When Applicable)*
Known Personally Y / N	ID Type	Issued By	
ID Checked ☐	ID #	Exp. Date	
Notary Service Performed at:		
Witness Name/Address:	Witness Signature:	
		Record No.
Notes/Comments:		

Printed Name of Signer	Signer's Signature	Phone No.

Signer's Address

Notary Service(s) Performed ☐ Jurat ☐ Acknowledgment ☐ Oath	Date Notarized	Time AM PM	Fee Charged $
Other Details			

Name/Type of Document	Document Date	Right Thumb Print
		(When Applicable)
Known Personally Y / N	ID Type Issued By	
ID Checked ☐	ID # Exp. Date	
Notary Service Performed at:		
Witness Name/Address:	Witness Signature:	
		Record No.
Notes/Comments:		

Printed Name of Signer	Signer's Signature	Phone No.

Signer's Address

Notary Service(s) Performed ☐ Jurat ☐ Acknowledgment ☐ Oath	Date Notarized	Time AM PM	Fee Charged $
Other Details			

Name/Type of Document	Document Date	Right Thumb Print
		(When Applicable)
Known Personally Y / N	ID Type Issued By	
ID Checked ☐	ID # Exp. Date	
Notary Service Performed at:		
Witness Name/Address:	Witness Signature:	
		Record No.
Notes/Comments:		

Printed Name of Signer	Signer's Signature	Phone No.

Signer's Address

Notary Service(s) Performed ☐ Jurat ☐ Acknowledgment ☐ Oath	Date Notarized	Time AM PM	Fee Charged $
Other Details			

Name/Type of Document	Document Date	Right Thumb Print (When Applicable)
Known Personally Y / N	ID Type	Issued By	
ID Checked ☐	ID #	Exp. Date	
Notary Service Performed at:		
Witness Name/Address:	Witness Signature:	
		Record No.
Notes/Comments:		

Printed Name of Signer	Signer's Signature	Phone No.

Signer's Address

Notary Service(s) Performed ☐ Jurat ☐ Acknowledgment ☐ Oath	Date Notarized	Time AM PM	Fee Charged $
Other Details			

Name/Type of Document	Document Date	Right Thumb Print (When Applicable)
Known Personally Y / N	ID Type	Issued By	
ID Checked ☐	ID #	Exp. Date	
Notary Service Performed at:		
Witness Name/Address:	Witness Signature:	
		Record No.
Notes/Comments:		

Printed Name of Signer	Signer's Signature	Phone No.

Signer's Address

Notary Service(s) Performed ☐ Jurat ☐ Acknowledgment ☐ Oath	Date Notarized	Time ᴬᴹ ᴾᴹ	Fee Charged $

Other Details

Name/Type of Document	Document Date	Right Thumb Print *(When Applicable)*

Known Personally Y / N	ID Type	Issued By

ID Checked ☐	ID #	Exp. Date

Notary Service Performed at:

Witness Name/Address:	Witness Signature:

Record No.

Notes/Comments:

Printed Name of Signer	Signer's Signature	Phone No.

Signer's Address

Notary Service(s) Performed ☐ Jurat ☐ Acknowledgment ☐ Oath	Date Notarized	Time ᴬᴹ ᴾᴹ	Fee Charged $

Other Details

Name/Type of Document	Document Date	Right Thumb Print *(When Applicable)*

Known Personally Y / N	ID Type	Issued By

ID Checked ☐	ID #	Exp. Date

Notary Service Performed at:

Witness Name/Address:	Witness Signature:

Record No.

Notes/Comments:

Printed Name of Signer	Signer's Signature	Phone No.

Signer's Address

Notary Service(s) Performed ☐ Jurat ☐ Acknowledgment ☐ Oath	Date Notarized	Time AM PM	Fee Charged $

Other Details

Name/Type of Document	Document Date	Right Thumb Print *(When Applicable)*

Known Personally Y / N	ID Type	Issued By

ID Checked ☐	ID #	Exp. Date

Notary Service Performed at:

Witness Name/Address:	Witness Signature:

Record No.

Notes/Comments:

Printed Name of Signer	Signer's Signature	Phone No.

Signer's Address

Notary Service(s) Performed ☐ Jurat ☐ Acknowledgment ☐ Oath	Date Notarized	Time AM PM	Fee Charged $

Other Details

Name/Type of Document	Document Date	Right Thumb Print *(When Applicable)*

Known Personally Y / N	ID Type	Issued By

ID Checked ☐	ID #	Exp. Date

Notary Service Performed at:

Witness Name/Address:	Witness Signature:

Record No.

Notes/Comments:

Printed Name of Signer	Signer's Signature	Phone No.

Signer's Address

Notary Service(s) Performed ☐ Jurat ☐ Acknowledgment ☐ Oath	Date Notarized	Time AM PM	Fee Charged $

Other Details

Name/Type of Document	Document Date	Right Thumb Print *(When Applicable)*

Known Personally Y / N	ID Type	Issued By	

ID Checked ☐	ID #	Exp. Date	

Notary Service Performed at:

Witness Name/Address:	Witness Signature:	

Record No.

Notes/Comments:

Printed Name of Signer	Signer's Signature	Phone No.

Signer's Address

Notary Service(s) Performed ☐ Jurat ☐ Acknowledgment ☐ Oath	Date Notarized	Time AM PM	Fee Charged $

Other Details

Name/Type of Document	Document Date	Right Thumb Print *(When Applicable)*

Known Personally Y / N	ID Type	Issued By	

ID Checked ☐	ID #	Exp. Date	

Notary Service Performed at:

Witness Name/Address:	Witness Signature:	

Record No.

Notes/Comments:

Printed Name of Signer	Signer's Signature	Phone No.

Signer's Address

Notary Service(s) Performed ☐ Jurat ☐ Acknowledgment ☐ Oath	Date Notarized	Time AM PM	Fee Charged $
Other Details			

Name/Type of Document	Document Date	Right Thumb Print *(When Applicable)*

Known Personally Y / N	ID Type	Issued By	
ID Checked ☐	ID #	Exp. Date	
Notary Service Performed at:			
Witness Name/Address:	Witness Signature:		
		Record No.	
Notes/Comments:			

Printed Name of Signer	Signer's Signature	Phone No.

Signer's Address

Notary Service(s) Performed ☐ Jurat ☐ Acknowledgment ☐ Oath	Date Notarized	Time AM PM	Fee Charged $
Other Details			

Name/Type of Document	Document Date	Right Thumb Print *(When Applicable)*

Known Personally Y / N	ID Type	Issued By	
ID Checked ☐	ID #	Exp. Date	
Notary Service Performed at:			
Witness Name/Address:	Witness Signature:		
		Record No.	
Notes/Comments:			

Printed Name of Signer	Signer's Signature	Phone No.

Signer's Address

Notary Service(s) Performed ☐ Jurat ☐ Acknowledgment ☐ Oath	Date Notarized	Time AM PM	Fee Charged $
Other Details			

Name/Type of Document	Document Date	Right Thumb Print *(When Applicable)*
Known Personally Y / N	ID Type	Issued By	
ID Checked ☐	ID #	Exp. Date	
Notary Service Performed at:		
Witness Name/Address:	Witness Signature:	
Notes/Comments:		Record No.

Printed Name of Signer	Signer's Signature	Phone No.

Signer's Address

Notary Service(s) Performed ☐ Jurat ☐ Acknowledgment ☐ Oath	Date Notarized	Time AM PM	Fee Charged $
Other Details			

Name/Type of Document	Document Date	Right Thumb Print *(When Applicable)*
Known Personally Y / N	ID Type	Issued By	
ID Checked ☐	ID #	Exp. Date	
Notary Service Performed at:		
Witness Name/Address:	Witness Signature:	
Notes/Comments:		Record No.

Printed Name of Signer	Signer's Signature	Phone No.

Signer's Address

Notary Service(s) Performed ☐Jurat ☐Acknowledgment ☐Oath	Date Notarized	Time AM PM	Fee Charged $

Other Details

Name/Type of Document	Document Date	Right Thumb Print *(When Applicable)*

Known Personally Y / N	ID Type	Issued By

ID Checked ☐	ID #	Exp. Date

Notary Service Performed at:

Witness Name/Address:	Witness Signature:

Record No.

Notes/Comments:

Printed Name of Signer	Signer's Signature	Phone No.

Signer's Address

Notary Service(s) Performed ☐Jurat ☐Acknowledgment ☐Oath	Date Notarized	Time AM PM	Fee Charged $

Other Details

Name/Type of Document	Document Date	Right Thumb Print *(When Applicable)*

Known Personally Y / N	ID Type	Issued By

ID Checked ☐	ID #	Exp. Date

Notary Service Performed at:

Witness Name/Address:	Witness Signature:

Record No.

Notes/Comments:

Printed Name of Signer	Signer's Signature	Phone No.

Signer's Address

Notary Service(s) Performed ☐ Jurat ☐ Acknowledgment ☐ Oath	Date Notarized	Time ᴬᴹ ᴾᴹ	Fee Charged $
Other Details			

Name/Type of Document	Document Date	Right Thumb Print (When Applicable)
Known Personally Y / N	ID Type Issued By	
ID Checked ☐ ID #	Exp. Date	
Notary Service Performed at:		
Witness Name/Address:	Witness Signature:	Record No.
Notes/Comments:		

Printed Name of Signer	Signer's Signature	Phone No.

Signer's Address

Notary Service(s) Performed ☐ Jurat ☐ Acknowledgment ☐ Oath	Date Notarized	Time ᴬᴹ ᴾᴹ	Fee Charged $
Other Details			

Name/Type of Document	Document Date	Right Thumb Print (When Applicable)
Known Personally Y / N	ID Type Issued By	
ID Checked ☐ ID #	Exp. Date	
Notary Service Performed at:		
Witness Name/Address:	Witness Signature:	Record No.
Notes/Comments:		

Printed Name of Signer	Signer's Signature	Phone No.

Signer's Address

Notary Service(s) Performed ☐ Jurat ☐ Acknowledgment ☐ Oath	Date Notarized	Time AM PM	Fee Charged $
Other Details			

Name/Type of Document	Document Date	Right Thumb Print *(When Applicable)*
Known Personally Y / N	ID Type	Issued By	
ID Checked ☐	ID #	Exp. Date	
Notary Service Performed at:		
Witness Name/Address:	Witness Signature:	
Notes/Comments:		Record No.

Printed Name of Signer	Signer's Signature	Phone No.

Signer's Address

Notary Service(s) Performed ☐ Jurat ☐ Acknowledgment ☐ Oath	Date Notarized	Time AM PM	Fee Charged $
Other Details			

Name/Type of Document	Document Date	Right Thumb Print *(When Applicable)*
Known Personally Y / N	ID Type	Issued By	
ID Checked ☐	ID #	Exp. Date	
Notary Service Performed at:		
Witness Name/Address:	Witness Signature:	
Notes/Comments:		Record No.

Printed Name of Signer	Signer's Signature	Phone No.

Signer's Address

Notary Service(s) Performed ☐ Jurat ☐ Acknowledgment ☐ Oath	Date Notarized	Time ᴬᴹ ᴾᴹ	Fee Charged $

Other Details

Name/Type of Document	Document Date	Right Thumb Print *(When Applicable)*

| Known Personally Y / N | ID Type | Issued By | |

| ID Checked ☐ | ID # | Exp. Date | |

Notary Service Performed at:

| Witness Name/Address: | Witness Signature: | |

| | | Record No. |

Notes/Comments:

Printed Name of Signer	Signer's Signature	Phone No.

Signer's Address

Notary Service(s) Performed ☐ Jurat ☐ Acknowledgment ☐ Oath	Date Notarized	Time ᴬᴹ ᴾᴹ	Fee Charged $

Other Details

Name/Type of Document	Document Date	Right Thumb Print *(When Applicable)*

| Known Personally Y / N | ID Type | Issued By | |

| ID Checked ☐ | ID # | Exp. Date | |

Notary Service Performed at:

| Witness Name/Address: | Witness Signature: | |

| | | Record No. |

Notes/Comments:

Printed Name of Signer	Signer's Signature	Phone No.
Signer's Address		

Notary Service(s) Performed ☐ Jurat ☐ Acknowledgment ☐ Oath	Date Notarized	Time AM PM	Fee Charged $
Other Details			

Name/Type of Document	Document Date	Right Thumb Print *(When Applicable)*
Known Personally Y / N	ID Type	Issued By
ID Checked ☐	ID #	Exp. Date
Notary Service Performed at:		
Witness Name/Address:	Witness Signature:	
Notes/Comments:		Record No.

Printed Name of Signer	Signer's Signature	Phone No.
Signer's Address		

Notary Service(s) Performed ☐ Jurat ☐ Acknowledgment ☐ Oath	Date Notarized	Time AM PM	Fee Charged $
Other Details			

Name/Type of Document	Document Date	Right Thumb Print *(When Applicable)*
Known Personally Y / N	ID Type	Issued By
ID Checked ☐	ID #	Exp. Date
Notary Service Performed at:		
Witness Name/Address:	Witness Signature:	
Notes/Comments:		Record No.

Printed Name of Signer	Signer's Signature	Phone No.

Signer's Address

Notary Service(s) Performed ☐ Jurat ☐ Acknowledgment ☐ Oath	Date Notarized	Time AM PM	Fee Charged $

Other Details

Name/Type of Document	Document Date	Right Thumb Print
		(When Applicable)

Known Personally Y / N	ID Type	Issued By	

ID Checked ☐	ID #	Exp. Date	

Notary Service Performed at:

Witness Name/Address:	Witness Signature:	

Notes/Comments:

Record No.

Printed Name of Signer	Signer's Signature	Phone No.

Signer's Address

Notary Service(s) Performed ☐ Jurat ☐ Acknowledgment ☐ Oath	Date Notarized	Time AM PM	Fee Charged $

Other Details

Name/Type of Document	Document Date	Right Thumb Print
		(When Applicable)

Known Personally Y / N	ID Type	Issued By	

ID Checked ☐	ID #	Exp. Date	

Notary Service Performed at:

Witness Name/Address:	Witness Signature:	

Record No.

Notes/Comments:

Printed Name of Signer	Signer's Signature	Phone No.

Signer's Address

Notary Service(s) Performed ☐ Jurat ☐ Acknowledgment ☐ Oath	Date Notarized	Time AM PM	Fee Charged $
Other Details			

Name/Type of Document	Document Date	Right Thumb Print *(When Applicable)*
Known Personally Y / N ID Type Issued By		
ID Checked ☐ ID # Exp. Date		
Notary Service Performed at:		
Witness Name/Address: Witness Signature:		
Notes/Comments:		Record No.

Printed Name of Signer	Signer's Signature	Phone No.

Signer's Address

Notary Service(s) Performed ☐ Jurat ☐ Acknowledgment ☐ Oath	Date Notarized	Time AM PM	Fee Charged $
Other Details			

Name/Type of Document	Document Date	Right Thumb Print *(When Applicable)*
Known Personally Y / N ID Type Issued By		
ID Checked ☐ ID # Exp. Date		
Notary Service Performed at:		
Witness Name/Address: Witness Signature:		
Notes/Comments:		Record No.

Printed Name of Signer	Signer's Signature	Phone No.

Signer's Address

Notary Service(s) Performed ☐ Jurat ☐ Acknowledgment ☐ Oath	Date Notarized	Time AM PM	Fee Charged $
Other Details			

Name/Type of Document	Document Date	Right Thumb Print
		(When Applicable)

Known Personally Y / N	ID Type	Issued By	

ID Checked ☐	ID #	Exp. Date	

Notary Service Performed at:	

Witness Name/Address:	Witness Signature:	

Notes/Comments:	Record No.

Printed Name of Signer	Signer's Signature	Phone No.

Signer's Address

Notary Service(s) Performed ☐ Jurat ☐ Acknowledgment ☐ Oath	Date Notarized	Time AM PM	Fee Charged $
Other Details			

Name/Type of Document	Document Date	Right Thumb Print
		(When Applicable)

Known Personally Y / N	ID Type	Issued By	

ID Checked ☐	ID #	Exp. Date	

Notary Service Performed at:	

Witness Name/Address:	Witness Signature:	

Notes/Comments:	Record No.

Printed Name of Signer	Signer's Signature	Phone No.

Signer's Address

Notary Service(s) Performed ☐ Jurat ☐ Acknowledgment ☐ Oath	Date Notarized	Time AM PM	Fee Charged $

Other Details

Name/Type of Document	Document Date	Right Thumb Print *(When Applicable)*

Known Personally Y / N	ID Type	Issued By	

ID Checked ☐	ID #	Exp. Date	

Notary Service Performed at:

Witness Name/Address:	Witness Signature:	

Record No.

Notes/Comments:

Printed Name of Signer	Signer's Signature	Phone No.

Signer's Address

Notary Service(s) Performed ☐ Jurat ☐ Acknowledgment ☐ Oath	Date Notarized	Time AM PM	Fee Charged $

Other Details

Name/Type of Document	Document Date	Right Thumb Print *(When Applicable)*

Known Personally Y / N	ID Type	Issued By	

ID Checked ☐	ID #	Exp. Date	

Notary Service Performed at:

Witness Name/Address:	Witness Signature:	

Record No.

Notes/Comments:

Printed Name of Signer	Signer's Signature	Phone No.

Signer's Address

Notary Service(s) Performed ☐ Jurat ☐ Acknowledgment ☐ Oath Other Details	Date Notarized	Time ᴬᴹ ᴾᴹ	Fee Charged $

Name/Type of Document	Document Date	Right Thumb Print *(When Applicable)*
Known Personally Y / N ID Type	Issued By	
ID Checked ☐ ID #	Exp. Date	
Notary Service Performed at:		
Witness Name/Address:	Witness Signature:	
Notes/Comments:		Record No.

Printed Name of Signer	Signer's Signature	Phone No.

Signer's Address

Notary Service(s) Performed ☐ Jurat ☐ Acknowledgment ☐ Oath Other Details	Date Notarized	Time ᴬᴹ ᴾᴹ	Fee Charged $

Name/Type of Document	Document Date	Right Thumb Print *(When Applicable)*
Known Personally Y / N ID Type	Issued By	
ID Checked ☐ ID #	Exp. Date	
Notary Service Performed at:		
Witness Name/Address:	Witness Signature:	
Notes/Comments:		Record No.

Printed Name of Signer	Signer's Signature	Phone No.

Signer's Address

Notary Service(s) Performed ☐ Jurat ☐ Acknowledgment ☐ Oath	Date Notarized	Time AM PM	Fee Charged $
Other Details			

Name/Type of Document	Document Date	Right Thumb Print (When Applicable)
Known Personally Y / N	ID Type	Issued By	
ID Checked ☐	ID #	Exp. Date	
Notary Service Performed at:		
Witness Name/Address:	Witness Signature:	
Notes/Comments:		Record No.

Printed Name of Signer	Signer's Signature	Phone No.

Signer's Address

Notary Service(s) Performed ☐ Jurat ☐ Acknowledgment ☐ Oath	Date Notarized	Time AM PM	Fee Charged $
Other Details			

Name/Type of Document	Document Date	Right Thumb Print (When Applicable)
Known Personally Y / N	ID Type	Issued By	
ID Checked ☐	ID #	Exp. Date	
Notary Service Performed at:		
Witness Name/Address:	Witness Signature:	
Notes/Comments:		Record No.

Printed Name of Signer	Signer's Signature	Phone No.

Signer's Address

Notary Service(s) Performed ☐ Jurat ☐ Acknowledgment ☐ Oath	Date Notarized	Time ᴬᴹ ᴾᴹ	Fee Charged $

Other Details

Name/Type of Document	Document Date	Right Thumb Print *(When Applicable)*

Known Personally Y / N	ID Type	Issued By

ID Checked ☐	ID #	Exp. Date

Notary Service Performed at:

Witness Name/Address:	Witness Signature:

Record No.

Notes/Comments:

Printed Name of Signer	Signer's Signature	Phone No.

Signer's Address

Notary Service(s) Performed ☐ Jurat ☐ Acknowledgment ☐ Oath	Date Notarized	Time ᴬᴹ ᴾᴹ	Fee Charged $

Other Details

Name/Type of Document	Document Date	Right Thumb Print *(When Applicable)*

Known Personally Y / N	ID Type	Issued By

ID Checked ☐	ID #	Exp. Date

Notary Service Performed at:

Witness Name/Address:	Witness Signature:

Record No.

Notes/Comments:

Printed Name of Signer	Signer's Signature	Phone No.

Signer's Address

Notary Service(s) Performed ☐ Jurat ☐ Acknowledgment ☐ Oath	Date Notarized	Time AM PM	Fee Charged $

Other Details

Name/Type of Document	Document Date	Right Thumb Print *(When Applicable)*
Known Personally Y / N	ID Type	Issued By	
ID Checked ☐	ID #	Exp. Date	

Notary Service Performed at:

Witness Name/Address:	Witness Signature:	Record No.
Notes/Comments:		

Printed Name of Signer	Signer's Signature	Phone No.

Signer's Address

Notary Service(s) Performed ☐ Jurat ☐ Acknowledgment ☐ Oath	Date Notarized	Time AM PM	Fee Charged $

Other Details

Name/Type of Document	Document Date	Right Thumb Print *(When Applicable)*
Known Personally Y / N	ID Type	Issued By	
ID Checked ☐	ID #	Exp. Date	

Notary Service Performed at:

Witness Name/Address:	Witness Signature:	Record No.
Notes/Comments:		

Printed Name of Signer	Signer's Signature	Phone No.

Signer's Address

Notary Service(s) Performed ☐ Jurat ☐ Acknowledgment ☐ Oath	Date Notarized	Time ᴬᴹ ᴾᴹ	Fee Charged $
Other Details			

Name/Type of Document	Document Date	Right Thumb Print
		(When Applicable)

Known Personally Y / N	ID Type	Issued By	
ID Checked ☐	ID #	Exp. Date	

Notary Service Performed at:

Witness Name/Address:	Witness Signature:	
Notes/Comments:		Record No.

Printed Name of Signer	Signer's Signature	Phone No.

Signer's Address

Notary Service(s) Performed ☐ Jurat ☐ Acknowledgment ☐ Oath	Date Notarized	Time ᴬᴹ ᴾᴹ	Fee Charged $
Other Details			

Name/Type of Document	Document Date	Right Thumb Print
		(When Applicable)

Known Personally Y / N	ID Type	Issued By	
ID Checked ☐	ID #	Exp. Date	

Notary Service Performed at:

Witness Name/Address:	Witness Signature:	
Notes/Comments:		Record No.

Printed Name of Signer	Signer's Signature	Phone No.

Signer's Address

Notary Service(s) Performed ☐ Jurat ☐ Acknowledgment ☐ Oath	Date Notarized	Time AM PM	Fee Charged $
Other Details			

Name/Type of Document	Document Date	Right Thumb Print (When Applicable)
Known Personally Y / N	ID Type	Issued By	
ID Checked ☐	ID #	Exp. Date	
Notary Service Performed at:		
Witness Name/Address:	Witness Signature:	
Notes/Comments:		Record No.

Printed Name of Signer	Signer's Signature	Phone No.

Signer's Address

Notary Service(s) Performed ☐ Jurat ☐ Acknowledgment ☐ Oath	Date Notarized	Time AM PM	Fee Charged $
Other Details			

Name/Type of Document	Document Date	Right Thumb Print (When Applicable)
Known Personally Y / N	ID Type	Issued By	
ID Checked ☐	ID #	Exp. Date	
Notary Service Performed at:		
Witness Name/Address:	Witness Signature:	
Notes/Comments:		Record No.

Printed Name of Signer	Signer's Signature	Phone No.

Signer's Address

Notary Service(s) Performed ☐ Jurat ☐ Acknowledgment ☐ Oath	Date Notarized	Time AM PM	Fee Charged $

Other Details

Name/Type of Document	Document Date	Right Thumb Print *(When Applicable)*

Known Personally Y / N	ID Type	Issued By

ID Checked ☐	ID #	Exp. Date

Notary Service Performed at:

Witness Name/Address:	Witness Signature:

Record No.

Notes/Comments:

Printed Name of Signer	Signer's Signature	Phone No.

Signer's Address

Notary Service(s) Performed ☐ Jurat ☐ Acknowledgment ☐ Oath	Date Notarized	Time AM PM	Fee Charged $

Other Details

Name/Type of Document	Document Date	Right Thumb Print *(When Applicable)*

Known Personally Y / N	ID Type	Issued By

ID Checked ☐	ID #	Exp. Date

Notary Service Performed at:

Witness Name/Address:	Witness Signature:

Record No.

Notes/Comments:

Printed Name of Signer	Signer's Signature	Phone No.

Signer's Address

Notary Service(s) Performed ☐ Jurat ☐ Acknowledgment ☐ Oath	Date Notarized	Time AM PM	Fee Charged $
Other Details			

Name/Type of Document	Document Date	Right Thumb Print (When Applicable)
Known Personally Y / N ID Type	Issued By	
ID Checked ☐ ID #	Exp. Date	
Notary Service Performed at:		
Witness Name/Address:	Witness Signature:	
Notes/Comments:		Record No.

Printed Name of Signer	Signer's Signature	Phone No.

Signer's Address

Notary Service(s) Performed ☐ Jurat ☐ Acknowledgment ☐ Oath	Date Notarized	Time AM PM	Fee Charged $
Other Details			

Name/Type of Document	Document Date	Right Thumb Print (When Applicable)
Known Personally Y / N ID Type	Issued By	
ID Checked ☐ ID #	Exp. Date	
Notary Service Performed at:		
Witness Name/Address:	Witness Signature:	
Notes/Comments:		Record No.

Printed Name of Signer	Signer's Signature	Phone No.

Signer's Address

Notary Service(s) Performed ☐ Jurat ☐ Acknowledgment ☐ Oath	Date Notarized	Time ᴬᴹ ᴾᴹ	Fee Charged $
Other Details			

Name/Type of Document	Document Date	Right Thumb Print
		(When Applicable)

Known Personally Y / N	ID Type	Issued By	
ID Checked ☐	ID #	Exp. Date	

Notary Service Performed at:

Witness Name/Address:	Witness Signature:	
		Record No.

Notes/Comments:

Printed Name of Signer	Signer's Signature	Phone No.

Signer's Address

Notary Service(s) Performed ☐ Jurat ☐ Acknowledgment ☐ Oath	Date Notarized	Time ᴬᴹ ᴾᴹ	Fee Charged $
Other Details			

Name/Type of Document	Document Date	Right Thumb Print
		(When Applicable)

Known Personally Y / N	ID Type	Issued By	
ID Checked ☐	ID #	Exp. Date	

Notary Service Performed at:

Witness Name/Address:	Witness Signature:	
		Record No.

Notes/Comments:

Printed Name of Signer	Signer's Signature	Phone No.

Signer's Address

Notary Service(s) Performed ☐ Jurat ☐ Acknowledgment ☐ Oath	Date Notarized	Time AM PM	Fee Charged $
Other Details			

Name/Type of Document	Document Date	Right Thumb Print (When Applicable)
Known Personally Y / N	ID Type	Issued By	
ID Checked ☐	ID #	Exp. Date	
Notary Service Performed at:		
Witness Name/Address:	Witness Signature:	
		Record No.
Notes/Comments:		

Printed Name of Signer	Signer's Signature	Phone No.

Signer's Address

Notary Service(s) Performed ☐ Jurat ☐ Acknowledgment ☐ Oath	Date Notarized	Time AM PM	Fee Charged $
Other Details			

Name/Type of Document	Document Date	Right Thumb Print (When Applicable)
Known Personally Y / N	ID Type	Issued By	
ID Checked ☐	ID #	Exp. Date	
Notary Service Performed at:		
Witness Name/Address:	Witness Signature:	
		Record No.
Notes/Comments:		

Printed Name of Signer	Signer's Signature	Phone No.

Signer's Address

Notary Service(s) Performed ☐Jurat ☐Acknowledgment ☐Oath	Date Notarized	Time AM PM	Fee Charged $
Other Details			

Name/Type of Document	Document Date	Right Thumb Print (When Applicable)
Known Personally Y / N	ID Type	Issued By	
ID Checked ☐	ID #	Exp. Date	
Notary Service Performed at:		
Witness Name/Address:	Witness Signature:	
Notes/Comments:		Record No.

Printed Name of Signer	Signer's Signature	Phone No.

Signer's Address

Notary Service(s) Performed ☐Jurat ☐Acknowledgment ☐Oath	Date Notarized	Time AM PM	Fee Charged $
Other Details			

Name/Type of Document	Document Date	Right Thumb Print (When Applicable)
Known Personally Y / N	ID Type	Issued By	
ID Checked ☐	ID #	Exp. Date	
Notary Service Performed at:		
Witness Name/Address:	Witness Signature:	
Notes/Comments:		Record No.

Printed Name of Signer	Signer's Signature	Phone No.

Signer's Address

Notary Service(s) Performed ☐ Jurat ☐ Acknowledgment ☐ Oath	Date Notarized	Time AM PM	Fee Charged $
Other Details			

Name/Type of Document	Document Date	Right Thumb Print
		(When Applicable)

Known Personally Y / N	ID Type	Issued By	
ID Checked ☐	ID #	Exp. Date	
Notary Service Performed at:			
Witness Name/Address:		Witness Signature:	
Notes/Comments:			Record No.

Printed Name of Signer	Signer's Signature	Phone No.

Signer's Address

Notary Service(s) Performed ☐ Jurat ☐ Acknowledgment ☐ Oath	Date Notarized	Time AM PM	Fee Charged $
Other Details			

Name/Type of Document	Document Date	Right Thumb Print
		(When Applicable)

Known Personally Y / N	ID Type	Issued By	
ID Checked ☐	ID #	Exp. Date	
Notary Service Performed at:			
Witness Name/Address:		Witness Signature:	
Notes/Comments:			Record No.

Printed Name of Signer	Signer's Signature	Phone No.

Signer's Address

Notary Service(s) Performed ☐ Jurat ☐ Acknowledgment ☐ Oath	Date Notarized	Time AM PM	Fee Charged $

Other Details

Name/Type of Document	Document Date	Right Thumb Print *(When Applicable)*
Known Personally Y / N	ID Type	Issued By
ID Checked ☐	ID #	Exp. Date

Notary Service Performed at:

Witness Name/Address:	Witness Signature:

Record No.

Notes/Comments:

Printed Name of Signer	Signer's Signature	Phone No.

Signer's Address

Notary Service(s) Performed ☐ Jurat ☐ Acknowledgment ☐ Oath	Date Notarized	Time AM PM	Fee Charged $

Other Details

Name/Type of Document	Document Date	Right Thumb Print *(When Applicable)*
Known Personally Y / N	ID Type	Issued By
ID Checked ☐	ID #	Exp. Date

Notary Service Performed at:

Witness Name/Address:	Witness Signature:

Record No.

Notes/Comments:

Printed Name of Signer	Signer's Signature	Phone No.

Signer's Address

Notary Service(s) Performed ☐ Jurat ☐ Acknowledgment ☐ Oath	Date Notarized	Time AM PM	Fee Charged $

Other Details

Name/Type of Document	Document Date	Right Thumb Print *(When Applicable)*

Known Personally Y / N	ID Type	Issued By	

ID Checked ☐	ID #	Exp. Date	

Notary Service Performed at:

Witness Name/Address:	Witness Signature:	
Notes/Comments:		Record No.

Printed Name of Signer	Signer's Signature	Phone No.

Signer's Address

Notary Service(s) Performed ☐ Jurat ☐ Acknowledgment ☐ Oath	Date Notarized	Time AM PM	Fee Charged $

Other Details

Name/Type of Document	Document Date	Right Thumb Print *(When Applicable)*

Known Personally Y / N	ID Type	Issued By	

ID Checked ☐	ID #	Exp. Date	

Notary Service Performed at:

Witness Name/Address:	Witness Signature:	
Notes/Comments:		Record No.

Printed Name of Signer	Signer's Signature	Phone No.

Signer's Address

Notary Service(s) Performed ☐Jurat ☐Acknowledgment ☐Oath	Date Notarized	Time AM PM	Fee Charged $
Other Details			

Name/Type of Document	Document Date	Right Thumb Print
		(When Applicable)

Known Personally Y / N	ID Type	Issued By	

ID Checked ☐	ID #	Exp. Date	

Notary Service Performed at:	

Witness Name/Address:	Witness Signature:	

Notes/Comments:	Record No.

Printed Name of Signer	Signer's Signature	Phone No.

Signer's Address

Notary Service(s) Performed ☐Jurat ☐Acknowledgment ☐Oath	Date Notarized	Time AM PM	Fee Charged $
Other Details			

Name/Type of Document	Document Date	Right Thumb Print
		(When Applicable)

Known Personally Y / N	ID Type	Issued By	

ID Checked ☐	ID #	Exp. Date	

Notary Service Performed at:	

Witness Name/Address:	Witness Signature:	

Notes/Comments:	Record No.

Printed Name of Signer	Signer's Signature	Phone No.
Signer's Address		

Notary Service(s) Performed ☐ Jurat ☐ Acknowledgment ☐ Oath	Date Notarized	Time ᴬᴹ ᴾᴹ	Fee Charged $
Other Details			

Name/Type of Document	Document Date	Right Thumb Print (When Applicable)
Known Personally Y / N ID Type	Issued By	
ID Checked ☐ ID #	Exp. Date	
Notary Service Performed at:		
Witness Name/Address:	Witness Signature:	
		Record No.
Notes/Comments:		

Printed Name of Signer	Signer's Signature	Phone No.
Signer's Address		

Notary Service(s) Performed ☐ Jurat ☐ Acknowledgment ☐ Oath	Date Notarized	Time ᴬᴹ ᴾᴹ	Fee Charged $
Other Details			

Name/Type of Document	Document Date	Right Thumb Print (When Applicable)
Known Personally Y / N ID Type	Issued By	
ID Checked ☐ ID #	Exp. Date	
Notary Service Performed at:		
Witness Name/Address:	Witness Signature:	
		Record No.
Notes/Comments:		

Printed Name of Signer	Signer's Signature	Phone No.

Signer's Address

Notary Service(s) Performed ☐ Jurat ☐ Acknowledgment ☐ Oath

Other Details

Date Notarized	Time	AM	Fee Charged
		PM	$

Name/Type of Document	Document Date	Right Thumb Print
		(When Applicable)

Known Personally	ID Type	Issued By	
Y / N			

ID Checked ☐	ID #	Exp. Date	

Notary Service Performed at:

Witness Name/Address:	Witness Signature:	

		Record No.

Notes/Comments:

Printed Name of Signer	Signer's Signature	Phone No.

Signer's Address

Notary Service(s) Performed ☐ Jurat ☐ Acknowledgment ☐ Oath

Other Details

Date Notarized	Time	AM	Fee Charged
		PM	$

Name/Type of Document	Document Date	Right Thumb Print
		(When Applicable)

Known Personally	ID Type	Issued By	
Y / N			

ID Checked ☐	ID #	Exp. Date	

Notary Service Performed at:

Witness Name/Address:	Witness Signature:	

		Record No.

Notes/Comments:

Printed Name of Signer	Signer's Signature	Phone No.

Signer's Address

Notary Service(s) Performed ☐ Jurat ☐ Acknowledgment ☐ Oath	Date Notarized	Time AM PM	Fee Charged $

Other Details

Name/Type of Document	Document Date	Right Thumb Print *(When Applicable)*

Known Personally Y / N	ID Type	Issued By

ID Checked ☐	ID #	Exp. Date

Notary Service Performed at:

Witness Name/Address:	Witness Signature:

Record No.

Notes/Comments:

Printed Name of Signer	Signer's Signature	Phone No.

Signer's Address

Notary Service(s) Performed ☐ Jurat ☐ Acknowledgment ☐ Oath	Date Notarized	Time AM PM	Fee Charged $

Other Details

Name/Type of Document	Document Date	Right Thumb Print *(When Applicable)*

Known Personally Y / N	ID Type	Issued By

ID Checked ☐	ID #	Exp. Date

Notary Service Performed at:

Witness Name/Address:	Witness Signature:

Record No.

Notes/Comments:

Printed Name of Signer	Signer's Signature	Phone No.

Signer's Address

Notary Service(s) Performed ☐ Jurat ☐ Acknowledgment ☐ Oath	Date Notarized	Time AM PM	Fee Charged $
Other Details			

Name/Type of Document	Document Date	Right Thumb Print
		(When Applicable)

Known Personally Y / N	ID Type	Issued By	

ID Checked ☐	ID #	Exp. Date	

Notary Service Performed at:

Witness Name/Address:	Witness Signature:	
		Record No.

Notes/Comments:

Printed Name of Signer	Signer's Signature	Phone No.

Signer's Address

Notary Service(s) Performed ☐ Jurat ☐ Acknowledgment ☐ Oath	Date Notarized	Time AM PM	Fee Charged $
Other Details			

Name/Type of Document	Document Date	Right Thumb Print
		(When Applicable)

Known Personally Y / N	ID Type	Issued By	

ID Checked ☐	ID #	Exp. Date	

Notary Service Performed at:

Witness Name/Address:	Witness Signature:	
		Record No.

Notes/Comments:

Printed Name of Signer	Signer's Signature	Phone No.

Signer's Address

Notary Service(s) Performed ☐ Jurat ☐ Acknowledgment ☐ Oath	Date Notarized	Time AM PM	Fee Charged $

Other Details

Name/Type of Document	Document Date	Right Thumb Print *(When Applicable)*

Known Personally Y / N	ID Type	Issued By	

ID Checked ☐	ID #	Exp. Date	

Notary Service Performed at:

Witness Name/Address:	Witness Signature:	

Record No.

Notes/Comments:

Printed Name of Signer	Signer's Signature	Phone No.

Signer's Address

Notary Service(s) Performed ☐ Jurat ☐ Acknowledgment ☐ Oath	Date Notarized	Time AM PM	Fee Charged $

Other Details

Name/Type of Document	Document Date	Right Thumb Print *(When Applicable)*

Known Personally Y / N	ID Type	Issued By	

ID Checked ☐	ID #	Exp. Date	

Notary Service Performed at:

Witness Name/Address:	Witness Signature:	

Record No.

Notes/Comments:

Printed Name of Signer	Signer's Signature	Phone No.

Signer's Address

Notary Service(s) Performed ☐ Jurat ☐ Acknowledgment ☐ Oath	Date Notarized	Time ᴬᴹ ᴾᴹ	Fee Charged $
Other Details			

Name/Type of Document	Document Date	Right Thumb Print *(When Applicable)*
Known Personally Y / N	ID Type	Issued By	
ID Checked ☐	ID #	Exp. Date	
Notary Service Performed at:		
Witness Name/Address:	Witness Signature:	
Notes/Comments:		Record No.

Printed Name of Signer	Signer's Signature	Phone No.

Signer's Address

Notary Service(s) Performed ☐ Jurat ☐ Acknowledgment ☐ Oath	Date Notarized	Time ᴬᴹ ᴾᴹ	Fee Charged $
Other Details			

Name/Type of Document	Document Date	Right Thumb Print *(When Applicable)*
Known Personally Y / N	ID Type	Issued By	
ID Checked ☐	ID #	Exp. Date	
Notary Service Performed at:		
Witness Name/Address:	Witness Signature:	
Notes/Comments:		Record No.

Printed Name of Signer	Signer's Signature	Phone No.

Signer's Address

Notary Service(s) Performed ☐ Jurat ☐ Acknowledgment ☐ Oath	Date Notarized	Time AM PM	Fee Charged $
Other Details			

Name/Type of Document	Document Date	Right Thumb Print (When Applicable)
Known Personally Y / N	ID Type	Issued By
ID Checked ☐	ID #	Exp. Date
Notary Service Performed at:		
Witness Name/Address:	Witness Signature:	
		Record No.
Notes/Comments:		

Printed Name of Signer	Signer's Signature	Phone No.

Signer's Address

Notary Service(s) Performed ☐ Jurat ☐ Acknowledgment ☐ Oath	Date Notarized	Time AM PM	Fee Charged $
Other Details			

Name/Type of Document	Document Date	Right Thumb Print (When Applicable)
Known Personally Y / N	ID Type	Issued By
ID Checked ☐	ID #	Exp. Date
Notary Service Performed at:		
Witness Name/Address:	Witness Signature:	
		Record No.
Notes/Comments:		

Printed Name of Signer	Signer's Signature	Phone No.

Signer's Address

Notary Service(s) Performed ☐ Jurat ☐ Acknowledgment ☐ Oath	Date Notarized	Time AM PM	Fee Charged $

Other Details

Name/Type of Document	Document Date	Right Thumb Print *(When Applicable)*

Known Personally Y / N	ID Type	Issued By	

ID Checked ☐	ID #	Exp. Date	

Notary Service Performed at:

Witness Name/Address:	Witness Signature:	

Record No.

Notes/Comments:

Printed Name of Signer	Signer's Signature	Phone No.

Signer's Address

Notary Service(s) Performed ☐ Jurat ☐ Acknowledgment ☐ Oath	Date Notarized	Time AM PM	Fee Charged $

Other Details

Name/Type of Document	Document Date	Right Thumb Print *(When Applicable)*

Known Personally Y / N	ID Type	Issued By	

ID Checked ☐	ID #	Exp. Date	

Notary Service Performed at:

Witness Name/Address:	Witness Signature:	

Record No.

Notes/Comments:

Printed Name of Signer	Signer's Signature	Phone No.

Signer's Address

Notary Service(s) Performed ☐ Jurat ☐ Acknowledgment ☐ Oath	Date Notarized	Time AM	Fee Charged
Other Details		PM	$

Name/Type of Document	Document Date	Right Thumb Print
		(When Applicable)
Known Personally Y / N	ID Type	Issued By	
ID Checked ☐	ID #	Exp. Date	
Notary Service Performed at:			
Witness Name/Address:	Witness Signature:		
Notes/Comments:		Record No.	

Printed Name of Signer	Signer's Signature	Phone No.

Signer's Address

Notary Service(s) Performed ☐ Jurat ☐ Acknowledgment ☐ Oath	Date Notarized	Time AM	Fee Charged
Other Details		PM	$

Name/Type of Document	Document Date	Right Thumb Print
		(When Applicable)
Known Personally Y / N	ID Type	Issued By	
ID Checked ☐	ID #	Exp. Date	
Notary Service Performed at:			
Witness Name/Address:	Witness Signature:		
Notes/Comments:		Record No.	

Printed Name of Signer	Signer's Signature	Phone No.

Signer's Address

Notary Service(s) Performed ☐ Jurat ☐ Acknowledgment ☐ Oath	Date Notarized	Time AM PM	Fee Charged $

Other Details

Name/Type of Document	Document Date	Right Thumb Print *(When Applicable)*

Known Personally Y / N	ID Type	Issued By

ID Checked ☐	ID #	Exp. Date

Notary Service Performed at:

Witness Name/Address:	Witness Signature:

Record No.

Notes/Comments:

Printed Name of Signer	Signer's Signature	Phone No.

Signer's Address

Notary Service(s) Performed ☐ Jurat ☐ Acknowledgment ☐ Oath	Date Notarized	Time AM PM	Fee Charged $

Other Details

Name/Type of Document	Document Date	Right Thumb Print *(When Applicable)*

Known Personally Y / N	ID Type	Issued By

ID Checked ☐	ID #	Exp. Date

Notary Service Performed at:

Witness Name/Address:	Witness Signature:

Record No.

Notes/Comments:

Printed Name of Signer	Signer's Signature	Phone No.

Signer's Address

Notary Service(s) Performed ☐ Jurat ☐ Acknowledgment ☐ Oath	Date Notarized	Time AM PM	Fee Charged $

Other Details

Name/Type of Document	Document Date	Right Thumb Print
		(When Applicable)

Known Personally Y / N	ID Type	Issued By	

ID Checked ☐	ID #	Exp. Date	

Notary Service Performed at:

Witness Name/Address:	Witness Signature:	
Notes/Comments:		**Record No.**

Printed Name of Signer	Signer's Signature	Phone No.

Signer's Address

Notary Service(s) Performed ☐ Jurat ☐ Acknowledgment ☐ Oath	Date Notarized	Time AM PM	Fee Charged $

Other Details

Name/Type of Document	Document Date	Right Thumb Print
		(When Applicable)

Known Personally Y / N	ID Type	Issued By	

ID Checked ☐	ID #	Exp. Date	

Notary Service Performed at:

Witness Name/Address:	Witness Signature:	
Notes/Comments:		**Record No.**

Printed Name of Signer	Signer's Signature	Phone No.

Signer's Address

Notary Service(s) Performed ☐ Jurat ☐ Acknowledgment ☐ Oath	Date Notarized	Time AM PM	Fee Charged $

Other Details

Name/Type of Document	Document Date	Right Thumb Print *(When Applicable)*

Known Personally Y / N	ID Type	Issued By

ID Checked ☐	ID #	Exp. Date

Notary Service Performed at:

Witness Name/Address:	Witness Signature:

Record No.

Notes/Comments:

Printed Name of Signer	Signer's Signature	Phone No.

Signer's Address

Notary Service(s) Performed ☐ Jurat ☐ Acknowledgment ☐ Oath	Date Notarized	Time AM PM	Fee Charged $

Other Details

Name/Type of Document	Document Date	Right Thumb Print *(When Applicable)*

Known Personally Y / N	ID Type	Issued By

ID Checked ☐	ID #	Exp. Date

Notary Service Performed at:

Witness Name/Address:	Witness Signature:

Record No.

Notes/Comments:

Printed Name of Signer	Signer's Signature	Phone No.

Signer's Address

Notary Service(s) Performed ☐ Jurat ☐ Acknowledgment ☐ Oath	Date Notarized	Time AM PM	Fee Charged $
Other Details			

Name/Type of Document	Document Date	Right Thumb Print *(When Applicable)*
Known Personally Y / N	ID Type	Issued By	
ID Checked ☐	ID #	Exp. Date	

Notary Service Performed at:

Witness Name/Address:	Witness Signature:	
Notes/Comments:		Record No.

Printed Name of Signer	Signer's Signature	Phone No.

Signer's Address

Notary Service(s) Performed ☐ Jurat ☐ Acknowledgment ☐ Oath	Date Notarized	Time AM PM	Fee Charged $
Other Details			

Name/Type of Document	Document Date	Right Thumb Print *(When Applicable)*
Known Personally Y / N	ID Type	Issued By	
ID Checked ☐	ID #	Exp. Date	

Notary Service Performed at:

Witness Name/Address:	Witness Signature:	
Notes/Comments:		Record No.

Printed Name of Signer	Signer's Signature	Phone No.

Signer's Address

Notary Service(s) Performed ☐ Jurat ☐ Acknowledgment ☐ Oath	Date Notarized	Time AM PM	Fee Charged $

Other Details

Name/Type of Document	Document Date	Right Thumb Print *(When Applicable)*

Known Personally Y / N	ID Type	Issued By	

ID Checked ☐	ID #	Exp. Date	

Notary Service Performed at:

Witness Name/Address:	Witness Signature:	

Record No.

Notes/Comments:

Printed Name of Signer	Signer's Signature	Phone No.

Signer's Address

Notary Service(s) Performed ☐ Jurat ☐ Acknowledgment ☐ Oath	Date Notarized	Time AM PM	Fee Charged $

Other Details

Name/Type of Document	Document Date	Right Thumb Print *(When Applicable)*

Known Personally Y / N	ID Type	Issued By	

ID Checked ☐	ID #	Exp. Date	

Notary Service Performed at:

Witness Name/Address:	Witness Signature:	

Record No.

Notes/Comments:

Printed Name of Signer	Signer's Signature	Phone No.

Signer's Address

Notary Service(s) Performed ☐ Jurat ☐ Acknowledgment ☐ Oath	Date Notarized	Time AM PM	Fee Charged $
Other Details			

Name/Type of Document	Document Date	Right Thumb Print *(When Applicable)*
Known Personally Y / N ID Type	Issued By	
ID Checked ☐ ID #	Exp. Date	
Notary Service Performed at:		
Witness Name/Address:	Witness Signature:	
Notes/Comments:		Record No.

Printed Name of Signer	Signer's Signature	Phone No.

Signer's Address

Notary Service(s) Performed ☐ Jurat ☐ Acknowledgment ☐ Oath	Date Notarized	Time AM PM	Fee Charged $
Other Details			

Name/Type of Document	Document Date	Right Thumb Print *(When Applicable)*
Known Personally Y / N ID Type	Issued By	
ID Checked ☐ ID #	Exp. Date	
Notary Service Performed at:		
Witness Name/Address:	Witness Signature:	
Notes/Comments:		Record No.

Printed Name of Signer	Signer's Signature	Phone No.

Signer's Address

Notary Service(s) Performed ☐ Jurat ☐ Acknowledgment ☐ Oath	Date Notarized	Time ᴬᴹ ᴾᴹ	Fee Charged $
Other Details			

Name/Type of Document	Document Date	Right Thumb Print
		(When Applicable)

Known Personally Y / N	ID Type	Issued By	

ID Checked ☐	ID #	Exp. Date	

Notary Service Performed at:

Witness Name/Address:	Witness Signature:	

		Record No.

Notes/Comments:

Printed Name of Signer	Signer's Signature	Phone No.

Signer's Address

Notary Service(s) Performed ☐ Jurat ☐ Acknowledgment ☐ Oath	Date Notarized	Time ᴬᴹ ᴾᴹ	Fee Charged $
Other Details			

Name/Type of Document	Document Date	Right Thumb Print
		(When Applicable)

Known Personally Y / N	ID Type	Issued By	

ID Checked ☐	ID #	Exp. Date	

Notary Service Performed at:

Witness Name/Address:	Witness Signature:	

		Record No.

Notes/Comments:

Printed Name of Signer	Signer's Signature	Phone No.

Signer's Address

Notary Service(s) Performed ☐ Jurat ☐ Acknowledgment ☐ Oath	Date Notarized	Time AM PM	Fee Charged $

Other Details

Name/Type of Document	Document Date	Right Thumb Print *(When Applicable)*
Known Personally Y / N	ID Type	Issued By	
ID Checked ☐	ID #	Exp. Date	

Notary Service Performed at:

Witness Name/Address:	Witness Signature:	
		Record No.

Notes/Comments:

Printed Name of Signer	Signer's Signature	Phone No.

Signer's Address

Notary Service(s) Performed ☐ Jurat ☐ Acknowledgment ☐ Oath	Date Notarized	Time AM PM	Fee Charged $

Other Details

Name/Type of Document	Document Date	Right Thumb Print *(When Applicable)*
Known Personally Y / N	ID Type	Issued By	
ID Checked ☐	ID #	Exp. Date	

Notary Service Performed at:

Witness Name/Address:	Witness Signature:	
		Record No.

Notes/Comments:

Printed Name of Signer	Signer's Signature	Phone No.

Signer's Address

Notary Service(s) Performed ☐ Jurat ☐ Acknowledgment ☐ Oath	Date Notarized	Time ᴬᴹ ᴾᴹ	Fee Charged $

Other Details

Name/Type of Document	Document Date	Right Thumb Print *(When Applicable)*
Known Personally Y / N ID Type	Issued By	
ID Checked ☐ ID #	Exp. Date	

Notary Service Performed at:

Witness Name/Address:	Witness Signature:	
		Record No.

Notes/Comments:

Printed Name of Signer	Signer's Signature	Phone No.

Signer's Address

Notary Service(s) Performed ☐ Jurat ☐ Acknowledgment ☐ Oath	Date Notarized	Time ᴬᴹ ᴾᴹ	Fee Charged $

Other Details

Name/Type of Document	Document Date	Right Thumb Print *(When Applicable)*
Known Personally Y / N ID Type	Issued By	
ID Checked ☐ ID #	Exp. Date	

Notary Service Performed at:

Witness Name/Address:	Witness Signature:	
		Record No.

Notes/Comments:

Printed Name of Signer	Signer's Signature	Phone No.

Signer's Address

Notary Service(s) Performed ☐ Jurat ☐ Acknowledgment ☐ Oath	Date Notarized	Time ᴬᴹ ᴾᴹ	Fee Charged $
Other Details			

Name/Type of Document	Document Date	Right Thumb Print *(When Applicable)*
Known Personally Y / N ID Type	Issued By	
ID Checked ☐ ID #	Exp. Date	
Notary Service Performed at:		
Witness Name/Address:	Witness Signature:	Record No.
Notes/Comments:		

Printed Name of Signer	Signer's Signature	Phone No.

Signer's Address

Notary Service(s) Performed ☐ Jurat ☐ Acknowledgment ☐ Oath	Date Notarized	Time ᴬᴹ ᴾᴹ	Fee Charged $
Other Details			

Name/Type of Document	Document Date	Right Thumb Print *(When Applicable)*
Known Personally Y / N ID Type	Issued By	
ID Checked ☐ ID #	Exp. Date	
Notary Service Performed at:		
Witness Name/Address:	Witness Signature:	Record No.
Notes/Comments:		

Printed Name of Signer	Signer's Signature	Phone No.

Signer's Address

Notary Service(s) Performed ☐ Jurat ☐ Acknowledgment ☐ Oath	Date Notarized	Time AM PM	Fee Charged $
Other Details			

Name/Type of Document	Document Date	Right Thumb Print (When Applicable)
Known Personally Y / N ID Type	Issued By	
ID Checked ☐ ID #	Exp. Date	
Notary Service Performed at:		
Witness Name/Address:	Witness Signature:	
		Record No.
Notes/Comments:		

Printed Name of Signer	Signer's Signature	Phone No.

Signer's Address

Notary Service(s) Performed ☐ Jurat ☐ Acknowledgment ☐ Oath	Date Notarized	Time AM PM	Fee Charged $
Other Details			

Name/Type of Document	Document Date	Right Thumb Print (When Applicable)
Known Personally Y / N ID Type	Issued By	
ID Checked ☐ ID #	Exp. Date	
Notary Service Performed at:		
Witness Name/Address:	Witness Signature:	
		Record No.
Notes/Comments:		

Printed Name of Signer	Signer's Signature	Phone No.

Signer's Address

Notary Service(s) Performed ☐ Jurat ☐ Acknowledgment ☐ Oath	Date Notarized	Time ᴬᴹ ᴾᴹ	Fee Charged $

Other Details

Name/Type of Document	Document Date	Right Thumb Print *(When Applicable)*

Known Personally Y / N	ID Type	Issued By	

ID Checked ☐	ID #	Exp. Date	

Notary Service Performed at:

Witness Name/Address:	Witness Signature:

Record No.

Notes/Comments:

Printed Name of Signer	Signer's Signature	Phone No.

Signer's Address

Notary Service(s) Performed ☐ Jurat ☐ Acknowledgment ☐ Oath	Date Notarized	Time ᴬᴹ ᴾᴹ	Fee Charged $

Other Details

Name/Type of Document	Document Date	Right Thumb Print *(When Applicable)*

Known Personally Y / N	ID Type	Issued By	

ID Checked ☐	ID #	Exp. Date	

Notary Service Performed at:

Witness Name/Address:	Witness Signature:

Record No.

Notes/Comments:

Printed Name of Signer	Signer's Signature	Phone No.

Signer's Address

Notary Service(s) Performed ☐ Jurat ☐ Acknowledgment ☐ Oath	Date Notarized	Time AM PM	Fee Charged $

Other Details

Name/Type of Document	Document Date	Right Thumb Print *(When Applicable)*
Known Personally Y / N	ID Type	Issued By
ID Checked ☐	ID #	Exp. Date

Notary Service Performed at:

Witness Name/Address:	Witness Signature:	

Notes/Comments:		Record No.

Printed Name of Signer	Signer's Signature	Phone No.

Signer's Address

Notary Service(s) Performed ☐ Jurat ☐ Acknowledgment ☐ Oath	Date Notarized	Time AM PM	Fee Charged $

Other Details

Name/Type of Document	Document Date	Right Thumb Print *(When Applicable)*
Known Personally Y / N	ID Type	Issued By
ID Checked ☐	ID #	Exp. Date

Notary Service Performed at:

Witness Name/Address:	Witness Signature:	

Notes/Comments:		Record No.

Printed Name of Signer	Signer's Signature	Phone No.

Signer's Address

Notary Service(s) Performed ☐ Jurat ☐ Acknowledgment ☐ Oath	Date Notarized	Time AM PM	Fee Charged $

Other Details

Name/Type of Document	Document Date	Right Thumb Print *(When Applicable)*

Known Personally Y / N	ID Type	Issued By

ID Checked ☐	ID #	Exp. Date

Notary Service Performed at:

Witness Name/Address:	Witness Signature:

Record No.

Notes/Comments:

Printed Name of Signer	Signer's Signature	Phone No.

Signer's Address

Notary Service(s) Performed ☐ Jurat ☐ Acknowledgment ☐ Oath	Date Notarized	Time AM PM	Fee Charged $

Other Details

Name/Type of Document	Document Date	Right Thumb Print *(When Applicable)*

Known Personally Y / N	ID Type	Issued By

ID Checked ☐	ID #	Exp. Date

Notary Service Performed at:

Witness Name/Address:	Witness Signature:

Record No.

Notes/Comments:

Printed Name of Signer	Signer's Signature	Phone No.

Signer's Address

Notary Service(s) Performed ☐ Jurat ☐ Acknowledgment ☐ Oath	Date Notarized	Time AM PM	Fee Charged $

Other Details

Name/Type of Document	Document Date	Right Thumb Print *(When Applicable)*
Known Personally Y / N	ID Type Issued By	
ID Checked ☐	ID # Exp. Date	

Notary Service Performed at:

Witness Name/Address:	Witness Signature:	
		Record No.

Notes/Comments:

Printed Name of Signer	Signer's Signature	Phone No.

Signer's Address

Notary Service(s) Performed ☐ Jurat ☐ Acknowledgment ☐ Oath	Date Notarized	Time AM PM	Fee Charged $

Other Details

Name/Type of Document	Document Date	Right Thumb Print *(When Applicable)*
Known Personally Y / N	ID Type Issued By	
ID Checked ☐	ID # Exp. Date	

Notary Service Performed at:

Witness Name/Address:	Witness Signature:	
		Record No.

Notes/Comments:

Printed Name of Signer	Signer's Signature	Phone No.

Signer's Address

Notary Service(s) Performed ☐ Jurat ☐ Acknowledgment ☐ Oath	Date Notarized	Time ᴬᴹ ᴾᴹ	Fee Charged $

Other Details

Name/Type of Document	Document Date	Right Thumb Print *(When Applicable)*

Known Personally Y / N	ID Type	Issued By	

ID Checked ☐	ID #	Exp. Date	

Notary Service Performed at:

Witness Name/Address:	Witness Signature:	

Notes/Comments:		Record No.

Printed Name of Signer	Signer's Signature	Phone No.

Signer's Address

Notary Service(s) Performed ☐ Jurat ☐ Acknowledgment ☐ Oath	Date Notarized	Time ᴬᴹ ᴾᴹ	Fee Charged $

Other Details

Name/Type of Document	Document Date	Right Thumb Print *(When Applicable)*

Known Personally Y / N	ID Type	Issued By	

ID Checked ☐	ID #	Exp. Date	

Notary Service Performed at:

Witness Name/Address:	Witness Signature:	

Notes/Comments:		Record No.

Printed Name of Signer	Signer's Signature	Phone No.

Signer's Address

Notary Service(s) Performed ☐ Jurat ☐ Acknowledgment ☐ Oath	Date Notarized	Time ᴬᴹ ᴾᴹ	Fee Charged $
Other Details			

Name/Type of Document	Document Date	Right Thumb Print (When Applicable)
Known Personally Y / N	ID Type	Issued By	
ID Checked ☐	ID #	Exp. Date	
Notary Service Performed at:			
Witness Name/Address:	Witness Signature:	
		Record No.
Notes/Comments:		

Printed Name of Signer	Signer's Signature	Phone No.

Signer's Address

Notary Service(s) Performed ☐ Jurat ☐ Acknowledgment ☐ Oath	Date Notarized	Time ᴬᴹ ᴾᴹ	Fee Charged $
Other Details			

Name/Type of Document	Document Date	Right Thumb Print (When Applicable)
Known Personally Y / N	ID Type	Issued By	
ID Checked ☐	ID #	Exp. Date	
Notary Service Performed at:			
Witness Name/Address:	Witness Signature:	
		Record No.
Notes/Comments:		

Printed Name of Signer	Signer's Signature	Phone No.

Signer's Address

Notary Service(s) Performed ☐ Jurat ☐ Acknowledgment ☐ Oath	Date Notarized	Time AM PM	Fee Charged $

Other Details

Name/Type of Document	Document Date	Right Thumb Print *(When Applicable)*

Known Personally Y / N	ID Type	Issued By	

ID Checked ☐	ID #	Exp. Date	

Notary Service Performed at:

Witness Name/Address:	Witness Signature:	

Notes/Comments:		Record No.

Printed Name of Signer	Signer's Signature	Phone No.

Signer's Address

Notary Service(s) Performed ☐ Jurat ☐ Acknowledgment ☐ Oath	Date Notarized	Time AM PM	Fee Charged $

Other Details

Name/Type of Document	Document Date	Right Thumb Print *(When Applicable)*

Known Personally Y / N	ID Type	Issued By	

ID Checked ☐	ID #	Exp. Date	

Notary Service Performed at:

Witness Name/Address:	Witness Signature:	

Notes/Comments:		Record No.

Printed Name of Signer	Signer's Signature	Phone No.

Signer's Address

Notary Service(s) Performed ☐ Jurat ☐ Acknowledgment ☐ Oath	Date Notarized	Time AM PM	Fee Charged $
Other Details			

Name/Type of Document	Document Date	Right Thumb Print
		(When Applicable)

Known Personally Y / N	ID Type	Issued By	
ID Checked ☐	ID #	Exp. Date	

Notary Service Performed at:

Witness Name/Address:	Witness Signature:	
		Record No.

Notes/Comments:

Printed Name of Signer	Signer's Signature	Phone No.

Signer's Address

Notary Service(s) Performed ☐ Jurat ☐ Acknowledgment ☐ Oath	Date Notarized	Time AM PM	Fee Charged $
Other Details			

Name/Type of Document	Document Date	Right Thumb Print
		(When Applicable)

Known Personally Y / N	ID Type	Issued By	
ID Checked ☐	ID #	Exp. Date	

Notary Service Performed at:

Witness Name/Address:	Witness Signature:	
		Record No.

Notes/Comments:

Printed Name of Signer	Signer's Signature	Phone No.
Signer's Address		

Notary Service(s) Performed ☐ Jurat ☐ Acknowledgment ☐ Oath	Date Notarized	Time AM PM	Fee Charged $
Other Details			

Name/Type of Document	Document Date	Right Thumb Print (When Applicable)
Known Personally Y / N	ID Type	Issued By	
ID Checked ☐	ID #	Exp. Date	
Notary Service Performed at:		
Witness Name/Address:	Witness Signature:	
		Record No.
Notes/Comments:		

Printed Name of Signer	Signer's Signature	Phone No.
Signer's Address		

Notary Service(s) Performed ☐ Jurat ☐ Acknowledgment ☐ Oath	Date Notarized	Time AM PM	Fee Charged $
Other Details			

Name/Type of Document	Document Date	Right Thumb Print (When Applicable)
Known Personally Y / N	ID Type	Issued By	
ID Checked ☐	ID #	Exp. Date	
Notary Service Performed at:		
Witness Name/Address:	Witness Signature:	
		Record No.
Notes/Comments:		

Printed Name of Signer	Signer's Signature	Phone No.
.		

Signer's Address

Notary Service(s) Performed ☐ Jurat ☐ Acknowledgment ☐ Oath	Date Notarized	Time AM PM	Fee Charged $
Other Details			

Name/Type of Document	Document Date	Right Thumb Print (When Applicable)
Known Personally Y / N	ID Type	Issued By
ID Checked ☐	ID #	Exp. Date
Notary Service Performed at:		
Witness Name/Address:	Witness Signature:	
		Record No.
Notes/Comments:		

Printed Name of Signer	Signer's Signature	Phone No.

Signer's Address

Notary Service(s) Performed ☐ Jurat ☐ Acknowledgment ☐ Oath	Date Notarized	Time AM PM	Fee Charged $
Other Details			

Name/Type of Document	Document Date	Right Thumb Print (When Applicable)
Known Personally Y / N	ID Type	Issued By
ID Checked ☐	ID #	Exp. Date
Notary Service Performed at:		
Witness Name/Address:	Witness Signature:	
		Record No.
Notes/Comments:		

Printed Name of Signer	Signer's Signature	Phone No.

Signer's Address

Notary Service(s) Performed ☐ Jurat ☐ Acknowledgment ☐ Oath	Date Notarized	Time AM PM	Fee Charged $
Other Details			

Name/Type of Document	Document Date	Right Thumb Print
Known Personally Y / N ID Type	Issued By	*(When Applicable)*
ID Checked ☐ ID #	Exp. Date	
Notary Service Performed at:		
Witness Name/Address: Witness Signature:		
		Record No.
Notes/Comments:		

Printed Name of Signer	Signer's Signature	Phone No.

Signer's Address

Notary Service(s) Performed ☐ Jurat ☐ Acknowledgment ☐ Oath	Date Notarized	Time AM PM	Fee Charged $
Other Details			

Name/Type of Document	Document Date	Right Thumb Print
Known Personally Y / N ID Type	Issued By	*(When Applicable)*
ID Checked ☐ ID #	Exp. Date	
Notary Service Performed at:		
Witness Name/Address: Witness Signature:		
		Record No.
Notes/Comments:		

Printed Name of Signer	Signer's Signature	Phone No.

Signer's Address

Notary Service(s) Performed ☐ Jurat ☐ Acknowledgment ☐ Oath	Date Notarized	Time ₐₘ PM	Fee Charged $
Other Details			

Name/Type of Document	Document Date	Right Thumb Print *(When Applicable)*
Known Personally ID Type Issued By Y / N		
ID Checked ☐ ID # Exp. Date		
Notary Service Performed at:		
Witness Name/Address: Witness Signature:		Record No.
Notes/Comments:		

Printed Name of Signer	Signer's Signature	Phone No.

Signer's Address

Notary Service(s) Performed ☐ Jurat ☐ Acknowledgment ☐ Oath	Date Notarized	Time ₐₘ PM	Fee Charged $
Other Details			

Name/Type of Document	Document Date	Right Thumb Print *(When Applicable)*
Known Personally ID Type Issued By Y / N		
ID Checked ☐ ID # Exp. Date		
Notary Service Performed at:		
Witness Name/Address: Witness Signature:		Record No.
Notes/Comments:		

Printed Name of Signer	Signer's Signature	Phone No.

Signer's Address

Notary Service(s) Performed ☐ Jurat ☐ Acknowledgment ☐ Oath	Date Notarized	Time ᴀᴍ ᴩᴍ	Fee Charged $

Other Details

Name/Type of Document	Document Date	Right Thumb Print *(When Applicable)*

Known Personally Y / N	ID Type	Issued By	

ID Checked ☐	ID #	Exp. Date	

Notary Service Performed at:

Witness Name/Address:	Witness Signature:	

Notes/Comments:		Record No.

Printed Name of Signer	Signer's Signature	Phone No.

Signer's Address

Notary Service(s) Performed ☐ Jurat ☐ Acknowledgment ☐ Oath	Date Notarized	Time ᴀᴍ ᴩᴍ	Fee Charged $

Other Details

Name/Type of Document	Document Date	Right Thumb Print *(When Applicable)*

Known Personally Y / N	ID Type	Issued By	

ID Checked ☐	ID #	Exp. Date	

Notary Service Performed at:

Witness Name/Address:	Witness Signature:	

Notes/Comments:		Record No.

Printed Name of Signer	Signer's Signature	Phone No.

Signer's Address

Notary Service(s) Performed ☐ Jurat ☐ Acknowledgment ☐ Oath	Date Notarized	Time ᴬᴹ ᴾᴹ	Fee Charged $

Other Details

Name/Type of Document	Document Date	Right Thumb Print *(When Applicable)*

Known Personally Y / N	ID Type	Issued By

ID Checked ☐	ID #	Exp. Date

Notary Service Performed at:

Witness Name/Address:	Witness Signature:

Record No.

Notes/Comments:

Printed Name of Signer	Signer's Signature	Phone No.

Signer's Address

Notary Service(s) Performed ☐ Jurat ☐ Acknowledgment ☐ Oath	Date Notarized	Time ᴬᴹ ᴾᴹ	Fee Charged $

Other Details

Name/Type of Document	Document Date	Right Thumb Print *(When Applicable)*

Known Personally Y / N	ID Type	Issued By

ID Checked ☐	ID #	Exp. Date

Notary Service Performed at:

Witness Name/Address:	Witness Signature:

Record No.

Notes/Comments:

Printed Name of Signer	Signer's Signature	Phone No.

Signer's Address

Notary Service(s) Performed ☐ Jurat ☐ Acknowledgment ☐ Oath	Date Notarized	Time AM PM	Fee Charged $

Other Details

Name/Type of Document	Document Date	Right Thumb Print *(When Applicable)*

Known Personally Y / N	ID Type	Issued By	

ID Checked ☐	ID #	Exp. Date	

Notary Service Performed at:

Witness Name/Address:	Witness Signature:	
		Record No.

Notes/Comments:

Printed Name of Signer	Signer's Signature	Phone No.

Signer's Address

Notary Service(s) Performed ☐ Jurat ☐ Acknowledgment ☐ Oath	Date Notarized	Time AM PM	Fee Charged $

Other Details

Name/Type of Document	Document Date	Right Thumb Print *(When Applicable)*

Known Personally Y / N	ID Type	Issued By	

ID Checked ☐	ID #	Exp. Date	

Notary Service Performed at:

Witness Name/Address:	Witness Signature:	
		Record No.

Notes/Comments:

Printed Name of Signer	Signer's Signature	Phone No.

Signer's Address

Notary Service(s) Performed ☐ Jurat ☐ Acknowledgment ☐ Oath	Date Notarized	Time AM PM	Fee Charged $
Other Details			

Name/Type of Document	Document Date	Right Thumb Print *(When Applicable)*
Known Personally Y / N	ID Type	Issued By	
ID Checked ☐	ID #	Exp. Date	
Notary Service Performed at:		
Witness Name/Address:	Witness Signature:	
		Record No.
Notes/Comments:		

Printed Name of Signer	Signer's Signature	Phone No.

Signer's Address

Notary Service(s) Performed ☐ Jurat ☐ Acknowledgment ☐ Oath	Date Notarized	Time AM PM	Fee Charged $
Other Details			

Name/Type of Document	Document Date	Right Thumb Print *(When Applicable)*
Known Personally Y / N	ID Type	Issued By	
ID Checked ☐	ID #	Exp. Date	
Notary Service Performed at:		
Witness Name/Address:	Witness Signature:	
		Record No.
Notes/Comments:		

Printed Name of Signer	Signer's Signature	Phone No.

Signer's Address

Notary Service(s) Performed ☐ Jurat ☐ Acknowledgment ☐ Oath	Date Notarized	Time AM PM	Fee Charged $

Other Details

Name/Type of Document	Document Date	Right Thumb Print
		(When Applicable)

Known Personally Y / N	ID Type	Issued By	

ID Checked ☐	ID #	Exp. Date	

Notary Service Performed at:

Witness Name/Address:	Witness Signature:	
		Record No.

Notes/Comments:

Printed Name of Signer	Signer's Signature	Phone No.

Signer's Address

Notary Service(s) Performed ☐ Jurat ☐ Acknowledgment ☐ Oath	Date Notarized	Time AM PM	Fee Charged $

Other Details

Name/Type of Document	Document Date	Right Thumb Print
		(When Applicable)

Known Personally Y / N	ID Type	Issued By	

ID Checked ☐	ID #	Exp. Date	

Notary Service Performed at:

Witness Name/Address:	Witness Signature:	
		Record No.

Notes/Comments:

Printed Name of Signer	Signer's Signature	Phone No.

Signer's Address

Notary Service(s) Performed ☐ Jurat ☐ Acknowledgment ☐ Oath	Date Notarized	Time AM PM	Fee Charged $

Other Details

Name/Type of Document	Document Date	Right Thumb Print *(When Applicable)*

Known Personally Y / N	ID Type	Issued By	

ID Checked ☐	ID #	Exp. Date	

Notary Service Performed at:

Witness Name/Address:	Witness Signature:	

		Record No.

Notes/Comments:

Printed Name of Signer	Signer's Signature	Phone No.

Signer's Address

Notary Service(s) Performed ☐ Jurat ☐ Acknowledgment ☐ Oath	Date Notarized	Time AM PM	Fee Charged $

Other Details

Name/Type of Document	Document Date	Right Thumb Print *(When Applicable)*

Known Personally Y / N	ID Type	Issued By	

ID Checked ☐	ID #	Exp. Date	

Notary Service Performed at:

Witness Name/Address:	Witness Signature:	

		Record No.

Notes/Comments:

Printed Name of Signer	Signer's Signature	Phone No.

Signer's Address

Notary Service(s) Performed ☐ Jurat ☐ Acknowledgment ☐ Oath	Date Notarized	Time AM PM	Fee Charged $
Other Details			

Name/Type of Document	Document Date	Right Thumb Print
		(When Applicable)

Known Personally Y / N	ID Type	Issued By	
ID Checked ☐	ID #	Exp. Date	

Notary Service Performed at:	

Witness Name/Address:	Witness Signature:	
		Record No.

Notes/Comments:

Printed Name of Signer	Signer's Signature	Phone No.

Signer's Address

Notary Service(s) Performed ☐ Jurat ☐ Acknowledgment ☐ Oath	Date Notarized	Time AM PM	Fee Charged $
Other Details			

Name/Type of Document	Document Date	Right Thumb Print
		(When Applicable)

Known Personally Y / N	ID Type	Issued By	
ID Checked ☐	ID #	Exp. Date	

Notary Service Performed at:	

Witness Name/Address:	Witness Signature:	
		Record No.

Notes/Comments:

Printed Name of Signer	Signer's Signature	Phone No.

Signer's Address

Notary Service(s) Performed ☐ Jurat ☐ Acknowledgment ☐ Oath	Date Notarized	Time AM PM	Fee Charged $
Other Details			

Name/Type of Document	Document Date	Right Thumb Print (When Applicable)

Known Personally Y / N	ID Type	Issued By	

ID Checked ☐	ID #	Exp. Date	

Notary Service Performed at:

Witness Name/Address:	Witness Signature:	
		Record No.

Notes/Comments:

Printed Name of Signer	Signer's Signature	Phone No.

Signer's Address

Notary Service(s) Performed ☐ Jurat ☐ Acknowledgment ☐ Oath	Date Notarized	Time AM PM	Fee Charged $
Other Details			

Name/Type of Document	Document Date	Right Thumb Print (When Applicable)

Known Personally Y / N	ID Type	Issued By	

ID Checked ☐	ID #	Exp. Date	

Notary Service Performed at:

Witness Name/Address:	Witness Signature:	
		Record No.

Notes/Comments:

Printed Name of Signer	Signer's Signature	Phone No.

Signer's Address

Notary Service(s) Performed ☐ Jurat ☐ Acknowledgment ☐ Oath	Date Notarized	Time AM PM	Fee Charged $

Other Details

Name/Type of Document	Document Date	Right Thumb Print (When Applicable)
Known Personally Y / N	ID Type	Issued By	
ID Checked ☐	ID #	Exp. Date	

Notary Service Performed at:

Witness Name/Address:	Witness Signature:	
		Record No.

Notes/Comments:

Printed Name of Signer	Signer's Signature	Phone No.

Signer's Address

Notary Service(s) Performed ☐ Jurat ☐ Acknowledgment ☐ Oath	Date Notarized	Time AM PM	Fee Charged $

Other Details

Name/Type of Document	Document Date	Right Thumb Print (When Applicable)
Known Personally Y / N	ID Type	Issued By	
ID Checked ☐	ID #	Exp. Date	

Notary Service Performed at:

Witness Name/Address:	Witness Signature:	
		Record No.

Notes/Comments:

Printed Name of Signer	Signer's Signature	Phone No.

Signer's Address

Notary Service(s) Performed ☐ Jurat ☐ Acknowledgment ☐ Oath	Date Notarized	Time AM PM	Fee Charged $
Other Details			

Name/Type of Document	Document Date	Right Thumb Print *(When Applicable)*
Known Personally Y / N ID Type	Issued By	
ID Checked ☐ ID #	Exp. Date	
Notary Service Performed at:		
Witness Name/Address:	Witness Signature:	
Notes/Comments:		Record No.

Printed Name of Signer	Signer's Signature	Phone No.

Signer's Address

Notary Service(s) Performed ☐ Jurat ☐ Acknowledgment ☐ Oath	Date Notarized	Time AM PM	Fee Charged $
Other Details			

Name/Type of Document	Document Date	Right Thumb Print *(When Applicable)*
Known Personally Y / N ID Type	Issued By	
ID Checked ☐ ID #	Exp. Date	
Notary Service Performed at:		
Witness Name/Address:	Witness Signature:	
Notes/Comments:		Record No.

Printed Name of Signer	Signer's Signature	Phone No.

Signer's Address

Notary Service(s) Performed ☐ Jurat ☐ Acknowledgment ☐ Oath	Date Notarized	Time ᴬᴹ ᴾᴹ	Fee Charged $

Other Details

Name/Type of Document	Document Date	Right Thumb Print (When Applicable)

Known Personally Y / N	ID Type	Issued By	

ID Checked ☐	ID #	Exp. Date	

Notary Service Performed at:

Witness Name/Address:	Witness Signature:	
		Record No.

Notes/Comments:

Printed Name of Signer	Signer's Signature	Phone No.

Signer's Address

Notary Service(s) Performed ☐ Jurat ☐ Acknowledgment ☐ Oath	Date Notarized	Time ᴬᴹ ᴾᴹ	Fee Charged $

Other Details

Name/Type of Document	Document Date	Right Thumb Print (When Applicable)

Known Personally Y / N	ID Type	Issued By	

ID Checked ☐	ID #	Exp. Date	

Notary Service Performed at:

Witness Name/Address:	Witness Signature:	
		Record No.

Notes/Comments:

Printed Name of Signer	Signer's Signature	Phone No.

Signer's Address

Notary Service(s) Performed ☐ Jurat ☐ Acknowledgment ☐ Oath	Date Notarized	Time AM PM	Fee Charged $
Other Details			

Name/Type of Document	Document Date	Right Thumb Print *(When Applicable)*
Known Personally Y / N	ID Type	Issued By	
ID Checked ☐	ID #	Exp. Date	
Notary Service Performed at:		
Witness Name/Address:	Witness Signature:	
Notes/Comments:		Record No.

Printed Name of Signer	Signer's Signature	Phone No.

Signer's Address

Notary Service(s) Performed ☐ Jurat ☐ Acknowledgment ☐ Oath	Date Notarized	Time AM PM	Fee Charged $
Other Details			

Name/Type of Document	Document Date	Right Thumb Print *(When Applicable)*
Known Personally Y / N	ID Type	Issued By	
ID Checked ☐	ID #	Exp. Date	
Notary Service Performed at:		
Witness Name/Address:	Witness Signature:	
Notes/Comments:		Record No.

Record 1

Printed Name of Signer	Signer's Signature	Phone No.

Signer's Address

Notary Service(s) Performed ☐ Jurat ☐ Acknowledgment ☐ Oath	Date Notarized	Time AM PM	Fee Charged $
Other Details			

Name/Type of Document	Document Date	Right Thumb Print *(When Applicable)*
Known Personally Y / N ID Type	Issued By	
ID Checked ☐ ID #	Exp. Date	
Notary Service Performed at:		
Witness Name/Address:	Witness Signature:	
Notes/Comments:		Record No.

Record 2

Printed Name of Signer	Signer's Signature	Phone No.

Signer's Address

Notary Service(s) Performed ☐ Jurat ☐ Acknowledgment ☐ Oath	Date Notarized	Time AM PM	Fee Charged $
Other Details			

Name/Type of Document	Document Date	Right Thumb Print *(When Applicable)*
Known Personally Y / N ID Type	Issued By	
ID Checked ☐ ID #	Exp. Date	
Notary Service Performed at:		
Witness Name/Address:	Witness Signature:	
Notes/Comments:		Record No.

Printed Name of Signer	Signer's Signature	Phone No.

Signer's Address

Notary Service(s) Performed ☐ Jurat ☐ Acknowledgment ☐ Oath	Date Notarized	Time AM PM	Fee Charged $
Other Details			

Name/Type of Document	Document Date	Right Thumb Print
		(When Applicable)

Known Personally Y / N	ID Type	Issued By	

ID Checked ☐	ID #	Exp. Date	

Notary Service Performed at:

Witness Name/Address:	Witness Signature:	

Notes/Comments:		Record No.

Printed Name of Signer	Signer's Signature	Phone No.

Signer's Address

Notary Service(s) Performed ☐ Jurat ☐ Acknowledgment ☐ Oath	Date Notarized	Time AM PM	Fee Charged $
Other Details			

Name/Type of Document	Document Date	Right Thumb Print
		(When Applicable)

Known Personally Y / N	ID Type	Issued By	

ID Checked ☐	ID #	Exp. Date	

Notary Service Performed at:

Witness Name/Address:	Witness Signature:	

Notes/Comments:		Record No.

Printed Name of Signer	Signer's Signature	Phone No.

Signer's Address

Notary Service(s) Performed ☐ Jurat ☐ Acknowledgment ☐ Oath	Date Notarized	Time AM PM	Fee Charged $

Other Details

Name/Type of Document	Document Date	Right Thumb Print *(When Applicable)*

Known Personally Y / N	ID Type	Issued By

ID Checked ☐	ID #	Exp. Date

Notary Service Performed at:

Witness Name/Address:	Witness Signature:

Record No.

Notes/Comments:

Printed Name of Signer	Signer's Signature	Phone No.

Signer's Address

Notary Service(s) Performed ☐ Jurat ☐ Acknowledgment ☐ Oath	Date Notarized	Time AM PM	Fee Charged $

Other Details

Name/Type of Document	Document Date	Right Thumb Print *(When Applicable)*

Known Personally Y / N	ID Type	Issued By

ID Checked ☐	ID #	Exp. Date

Notary Service Performed at:

Witness Name/Address:	Witness Signature:

Record No.

Notes/Comments:

Printed Name of Signer	Signer's Signature	Phone No.

Signer's Address

Notary Service(s) Performed ☐ Jurat ☐ Acknowledgment ☐ Oath	Date Notarized	Time ᴬᴹ ᴾᴹ	Fee Charged $

Other Details

Name/Type of Document	Document Date	Right Thumb Print (When Applicable)

Known Personally Y / N	ID Type	Issued By

ID Checked ☐	ID #	Exp. Date

Notary Service Performed at:

Witness Name/Address:	Witness Signature:

Record No.

Notes/Comments:

Printed Name of Signer	Signer's Signature	Phone No.

Signer's Address

Notary Service(s) Performed ☐ Jurat ☐ Acknowledgment ☐ Oath	Date Notarized	Time ᴬᴹ ᴾᴹ	Fee Charged $

Other Details

Name/Type of Document	Document Date	Right Thumb Print (When Applicable)

Known Personally Y / N	ID Type	Issued By

ID Checked ☐	ID #	Exp. Date

Notary Service Performed at:

Witness Name/Address:	Witness Signature:

Record No.

Notes/Comments:

Printed Name of Signer	Signer's Signature	Phone No.

Signer's Address

Notary Service(s) Performed ☐ Jurat ☐ Acknowledgment ☐ Oath Other Details	Date Notarized	Time AM PM	Fee Charged $

Name/Type of Document	Document Date	Right Thumb Print *(When Applicable)*
Known Personally Y / N ID Type Issued By		
ID Checked ☐ ID # Exp. Date		
Notary Service Performed at:		
Witness Name/Address: Witness Signature:		Record No.
Notes/Comments:		

Printed Name of Signer	Signer's Signature	Phone No.

Signer's Address

Notary Service(s) Performed ☐ Jurat ☐ Acknowledgment ☐ Oath Other Details	Date Notarized	Time AM PM	Fee Charged $

Name/Type of Document	Document Date	Right Thumb Print *(When Applicable)*
Known Personally Y / N ID Type Issued By		
ID Checked ☐ ID # Exp. Date		
Notary Service Performed at:		
Witness Name/Address: Witness Signature:		Record No.
Notes/Comments:		

Printed Name of Signer	Signer's Signature	Phone No.

Signer's Address

Notary Service(s) Performed ☐ Jurat ☐ Acknowledgment ☐ Oath	Date Notarized	Time AM PM	Fee Charged $
Other Details			

Name/Type of Document	Document Date	Right Thumb Print *(When Applicable)*
Known Personally Y / N ID Type	Issued By	
ID Checked ☐ ID #	Exp. Date	
Notary Service Performed at:		
Witness Name/Address: Witness Signature:		
Notes/Comments:	Record No.	

Printed Name of Signer	Signer's Signature	Phone No.

Signer's Address

Notary Service(s) Performed ☐ Jurat ☐ Acknowledgment ☐ Oath	Date Notarized	Time AM PM	Fee Charged $
Other Details			

Name/Type of Document	Document Date	Right Thumb Print *(When Applicable)*
Known Personally Y / N ID Type	Issued By	
ID Checked ☐ ID #	Exp. Date	
Notary Service Performed at:		
Witness Name/Address: Witness Signature:		
Notes/Comments:	Record No.	

Printed Name of Signer	Signer's Signature	Phone No.

Signer's Address

Notary Service(s) Performed ☐ Jurat ☐ Acknowledgment ☐ Oath	Date Notarized	Time AM PM	Fee Charged $

Other Details

Name/Type of Document	Document Date	Right Thumb Print *(When Applicable)*

Known Personally Y / N	ID Type	Issued By	

ID Checked ☐	ID #	Exp. Date	

Notary Service Performed at:

Witness Name/Address:	Witness Signature:	

| | | Record No. |

Notes/Comments:

Printed Name of Signer	Signer's Signature	Phone No.

Signer's Address

Notary Service(s) Performed ☐ Jurat ☐ Acknowledgment ☐ Oath	Date Notarized	Time AM PM	Fee Charged $

Other Details

Name/Type of Document	Document Date	Right Thumb Print *(When Applicable)*

Known Personally Y / N	ID Type	Issued By	

ID Checked ☐	ID #	Exp. Date	

Notary Service Performed at:

Witness Name/Address:	Witness Signature:	

| | | Record No. |

Notes/Comments:

Printed Name of Signer	Signer's Signature	Phone No.

Signer's Address

Notary Service(s) Performed ☐ Jurat ☐ Acknowledgment ☐ Oath	Date Notarized	Time ᴬᴹ ᴾᴹ	Fee Charged $
Other Details			

Name/Type of Document	Document Date	Right Thumb Print (When Applicable)
Known Personally Y / N	ID Type	Issued By
ID Checked ☐	ID #	Exp. Date
Notary Service Performed at:		
Witness Name/Address:	Witness Signature:	
		Record No.
Notes/Comments:		

Printed Name of Signer	Signer's Signature	Phone No.

Signer's Address

Notary Service(s) Performed ☐ Jurat ☐ Acknowledgment ☐ Oath	Date Notarized	Time ᴬᴹ ᴾᴹ	Fee Charged $
Other Details			

Name/Type of Document	Document Date	Right Thumb Print (When Applicable)
Known Personally Y / N	ID Type	Issued By
ID Checked ☐	ID #	Exp. Date
Notary Service Performed at:		
Witness Name/Address:	Witness Signature:	
		Record No.
Notes/Comments:		

Printed Name of Signer	Signer's Signature	Phone No.

Signer's Address

Notary Service(s) Performed ☐ Jurat ☐ Acknowledgment ☐ Oath	Date Notarized	Time AM PM	Fee Charged $
Other Details			

Name/Type of Document	Document Date	Right Thumb Print (When Applicable)
Known Personally Y / N ID Type	Issued By	
ID Checked ☐ ID #	Exp. Date	
Notary Service Performed at:		
Witness Name/Address:	Witness Signature:	
		Record No.
Notes/Comments:		

Printed Name of Signer	Signer's Signature	Phone No.

Signer's Address

Notary Service(s) Performed ☐ Jurat ☐ Acknowledgment ☐ Oath	Date Notarized	Time AM PM	Fee Charged $
Other Details			

Name/Type of Document	Document Date	Right Thumb Print (When Applicable)
Known Personally Y / N ID Type	Issued By	
ID Checked ☐ ID #	Exp. Date	
Notary Service Performed at:		
Witness Name/Address:	Witness Signature:	
		Record No.
Notes/Comments:		

Printed Name of Signer	Signer's Signature	Phone No.

Signer's Address

Notary Service(s) Performed ☐ Jurat ☐ Acknowledgment ☐ Oath	Date Notarized	Time AM PM	Fee Charged $
Other Details			

Name/Type of Document	Document Date	Right Thumb Print *(When Applicable)*

Known Personally Y / N	ID Type	Issued By

ID Checked ☐	ID #	Exp. Date

Notary Service Performed at:

Witness Name/Address:	Witness Signature:

Record No.

Notes/Comments:

Printed Name of Signer	Signer's Signature	Phone No.

Signer's Address

Notary Service(s) Performed ☐ Jurat ☐ Acknowledgment ☐ Oath	Date Notarized	Time AM PM	Fee Charged $
Other Details			

Name/Type of Document	Document Date	Right Thumb Print *(When Applicable)*

Known Personally Y / N	ID Type	Issued By

ID Checked ☐	ID #	Exp. Date

Notary Service Performed at:

Witness Name/Address:	Witness Signature:

Record No.

Notes/Comments:

Printed Name of Signer	Signer's Signature	Phone No.

Signer's Address

Notary Service(s) Performed ☐ Jurat ☐ Acknowledgment ☐ Oath	Date Notarized	Time AM PM	Fee Charged $
Other Details			

Name/Type of Document	Document Date	Right Thumb Print (When Applicable)
Known Personally Y / N ID Type	Issued By	
ID Checked ☐ ID #	Exp. Date	
Notary Service Performed at:		
Witness Name/Address:	Witness Signature:	
		Record No.
Notes/Comments:		

Printed Name of Signer	Signer's Signature	Phone No.

Signer's Address

Notary Service(s) Performed ☐ Jurat ☐ Acknowledgment ☐ Oath	Date Notarized	Time AM PM	Fee Charged $
Other Details			

Name/Type of Document	Document Date	Right Thumb Print (When Applicable)
Known Personally Y / N ID Type	Issued By	
ID Checked ☐ ID #	Exp. Date	
Notary Service Performed at:		
Witness Name/Address:	Witness Signature:	
		Record No.
Notes/Comments:		

Printed Name of Signer	Signer's Signature	Phone No.

Signer's Address

Notary Service(s) Performed ☐ Jurat ☐ Acknowledgment ☐ Oath	Date Notarized	Time AM PM	Fee Charged $

Other Details

Name/Type of Document	Document Date	Right Thumb Print (When Applicable)

Known Personally Y / N	ID Type	Issued By

ID Checked ☐	ID #	Exp. Date

Notary Service Performed at:

Witness Name/Address:	Witness Signature:

Record No.

Notes/Comments:

Printed Name of Signer	Signer's Signature	Phone No.

Signer's Address

Notary Service(s) Performed ☐ Jurat ☐ Acknowledgment ☐ Oath	Date Notarized	Time AM PM	Fee Charged $

Other Details

Name/Type of Document	Document Date	Right Thumb Print (When Applicable)

Known Personally Y / N	ID Type	Issued By

ID Checked ☐	ID #	Exp. Date

Notary Service Performed at:

Witness Name/Address:	Witness Signature:

Record No.

Notes/Comments:

Printed Name of Signer	Signer's Signature	Phone No.

Signer's Address

Notary Service(s) Performed ☐ Jurat ☐ Acknowledgment ☐ Oath	Date Notarized	Time AM PM	Fee Charged $
Other Details			

Name/Type of Document	Document Date	Right Thumb Print (When Applicable)
Known Personally Y / N	ID Type	Issued By	
ID Checked ☐	ID #	Exp. Date	
Notary Service Performed at:			
Witness Name/Address:	Witness Signature:	
		Record No.
Notes/Comments:		

Printed Name of Signer	Signer's Signature	Phone No.

Signer's Address

Notary Service(s) Performed ☐ Jurat ☐ Acknowledgment ☐ Oath	Date Notarized	Time AM PM	Fee Charged $
Other Details			

Name/Type of Document	Document Date	Right Thumb Print (When Applicable)
Known Personally Y / N	ID Type	Issued By	
ID Checked ☐	ID #	Exp. Date	
Notary Service Performed at:			
Witness Name/Address:	Witness Signature:	
		Record No.
Notes/Comments:		

Printed Name of Signer	Signer's Signature	Phone No.

Signer's Address

Notary Service(s) Performed ☐ Jurat ☐ Acknowledgment ☐ Oath	Date Notarized	Time AM PM	Fee Charged $
Other Details			

Name/Type of Document	Document Date	Right Thumb Print (When Applicable)
Known Personally Y / N	ID Type	Issued By	
ID Checked ☐	ID #	Exp. Date	
Notary Service Performed at:		
Witness Name/Address:	Witness Signature:	
		Record No.
Notes/Comments:		

Printed Name of Signer	Signer's Signature	Phone No.

Signer's Address

Notary Service(s) Performed ☐ Jurat ☐ Acknowledgment ☐ Oath	Date Notarized	Time AM PM	Fee Charged $
Other Details			

Name/Type of Document	Document Date	Right Thumb Print (When Applicable)
Known Personally Y / N	ID Type	Issued By	
ID Checked ☐	ID #	Exp. Date	
Notary Service Performed at:		
Witness Name/Address:	Witness Signature:	
		Record No.
Notes/Comments:		

Printed Name of Signer	Signer's Signature	Phone No.

Signer's Address

Notary Service(s) Performed ☐ Jurat ☐ Acknowledgment ☐ Oath	Date Notarized	Time AM	Fee Charged
Other Details		PM	$

Name/Type of Document	Document Date	Right Thumb Print *(When Applicable)*

Known Personally Y / N	ID Type	Issued By	

ID Checked ☐	ID #	Exp. Date	

Notary Service Performed at:

Witness Name/Address:	Witness Signature:	
Notes/Comments:		Record No.

Printed Name of Signer	Signer's Signature	Phone No.

Signer's Address

Notary Service(s) Performed ☐ Jurat ☐ Acknowledgment ☐ Oath	Date Notarized	Time AM	Fee Charged
Other Details		PM	$

Name/Type of Document	Document Date	Right Thumb Print *(When Applicable)*

Known Personally Y / N	ID Type	Issued By	

ID Checked ☐	ID #	Exp. Date	

Notary Service Performed at:

Witness Name/Address:	Witness Signature:	
Notes/Comments:		Record No.

Printed Name of Signer	Signer's Signature	Phone No.

Signer's Address

Notary Service(s) Performed ☐ Jurat ☐ Acknowledgment ☐ Oath Other Details	Date Notarized	Time AM PM	Fee Charged $

Name/Type of Document	Document Date	Right Thumb Print *(When Applicable)*
Known Personally Y / N	ID Type	Issued By	
ID Checked ☐	ID #	Exp. Date	
Notary Service Performed at:		
Witness Name/Address:	Witness Signature:	
		Record No.
Notes/Comments:		

Printed Name of Signer	Signer's Signature	Phone No.

Signer's Address

Notary Service(s) Performed ☐ Jurat ☐ Acknowledgment ☐ Oath Other Details	Date Notarized	Time AM PM	Fee Charged $

Name/Type of Document	Document Date	Right Thumb Print *(When Applicable)*
Known Personally Y / N	ID Type	Issued By	
ID Checked ☐	ID #	Exp. Date	
Notary Service Performed at:		
Witness Name/Address:	Witness Signature:	
		Record No.
Notes/Comments:		

Printed Name of Signer	Signer's Signature	Phone No.

Signer's Address

Notary Service(s) Performed ☐ Jurat ☐ Acknowledgment ☐ Oath	Date Notarized	Time AM PM	Fee Charged $
Other Details			

Name/Type of Document	Document Date	Right Thumb Print (When Applicable)
Known Personally Y / N ID Type Issued By		
ID Checked ☐ ID # Exp. Date		
Notary Service Performed at:		
Witness Name/Address: Witness Signature:		
Notes/Comments:		Record No.

Printed Name of Signer	Signer's Signature	Phone No.

Signer's Address

Notary Service(s) Performed ☐ Jurat ☐ Acknowledgment ☐ Oath	Date Notarized	Time AM PM	Fee Charged $
Other Details			

Name/Type of Document	Document Date	Right Thumb Print (When Applicable)
Known Personally Y / N ID Type Issued By		
ID Checked ☐ ID # Exp. Date		
Notary Service Performed at:		
Witness Name/Address: Witness Signature:		
Notes/Comments:		Record No.

Printed Name of Signer	Signer's Signature	Phone No.

Signer's Address

Notary Service(s) Performed ☐ Jurat ☐ Acknowledgment ☐ Oath	Date Notarized	Time ᴬᴹ ᴾᴹ	Fee Charged $
Other Details			

Name/Type of Document	Document Date	Right Thumb Print
		(When Applicable)

Known Personally Y / N	ID Type	Issued By	
ID Checked ☐	ID #	Exp. Date	

Notary Service Performed at:

Witness Name/Address:	Witness Signature:	
		Record No.

Notes/Comments:

Printed Name of Signer	Signer's Signature	Phone No.

Signer's Address

Notary Service(s) Performed ☐ Jurat ☐ Acknowledgment ☐ Oath	Date Notarized	Time ᴬᴹ ᴾᴹ	Fee Charged $
Other Details			

Name/Type of Document	Document Date	Right Thumb Print
		(When Applicable)

Known Personally Y / N	ID Type	Issued By	
ID Checked ☐	ID #	Exp. Date	

Notary Service Performed at:

Witness Name/Address:	Witness Signature:	
		Record No.

Notes/Comments:

Printed Name of Signer	Signer's Signature	Phone No.

Signer's Address

Notary Service(s) Performed ☐ Jurat ☐ Acknowledgment ☐ Oath	Date Notarized	Time AM PM	Fee Charged $

Other Details

Name/Type of Document	Document Date	Right Thumb Print *(When Applicable)*

Known Personally Y / N	ID Type	Issued By	

ID Checked ☐	ID #	Exp. Date	

Notary Service Performed at:

Witness Name/Address:	Witness Signature:	

Record No.

Notes/Comments:

Printed Name of Signer	Signer's Signature	Phone No.

Signer's Address

Notary Service(s) Performed ☐ Jurat ☐ Acknowledgment ☐ Oath	Date Notarized	Time AM PM	Fee Charged $

Other Details

Name/Type of Document	Document Date	Right Thumb Print *(When Applicable)*

Known Personally Y / N	ID Type	Issued By	

ID Checked ☐	ID #	Exp. Date	

Notary Service Performed at:

Witness Name/Address:	Witness Signature:	

Record No.

Notes/Comments:

Printed Name of Signer	Signer's Signature	Phone No.

Signer's Address

Notary Service(s) Performed ☐ Jurat ☐ Acknowledgment ☐ Oath	Date Notarized	Time ᴬᴹ ᴾᴹ	Fee Charged $
Other Details			

Name/Type of Document	Document Date	Right Thumb Print *(When Applicable)*
Known Personally Y / N ID Type	Issued By	
ID Checked ☐ ID #	Exp. Date	
Notary Service Performed at:		
Witness Name/Address:	Witness Signature:	
Notes/Comments:		Record No.

Printed Name of Signer	Signer's Signature	Phone No.

Signer's Address

Notary Service(s) Performed ☐ Jurat ☐ Acknowledgment ☐ Oath	Date Notarized	Time ᴬᴹ ᴾᴹ	Fee Charged $
Other Details			

Name/Type of Document	Document Date	Right Thumb Print *(When Applicable)*
Known Personally Y / N ID Type	Issued By	
ID Checked ☐ ID #	Exp. Date	
Notary Service Performed at:		
Witness Name/Address:	Witness Signature:	
Notes/Comments:		Record No.

Printed Name of Signer	Signer's Signature	Phone No.

Signer's Address

Notary Service(s) Performed ☐ Jurat ☐ Acknowledgment ☐ Oath	Date Notarized	Time AM PM	Fee Charged $

Other Details

Name/Type of Document	Document Date	Right Thumb Print (When Applicable)

Known Personally Y / N	ID Type	Issued By

ID Checked ☐	ID #	Exp. Date

Notary Service Performed at:

Witness Name/Address:	Witness Signature:

Record No.

Notes/Comments:

Printed Name of Signer	Signer's Signature	Phone No.

Signer's Address

Notary Service(s) Performed ☐ Jurat ☐ Acknowledgment ☐ Oath	Date Notarized	Time AM PM	Fee Charged $

Other Details

Name/Type of Document	Document Date	Right Thumb Print (When Applicable)

Known Personally Y / N	ID Type	Issued By

ID Checked ☐	ID #	Exp. Date

Notary Service Performed at:

Witness Name/Address:	Witness Signature:

Record No.

Notes/Comments:

Printed Name of Signer	Signer's Signature	Phone No.

Signer's Address

Notary Service(s) Performed ☐ Jurat ☐ Acknowledgment ☐ Oath	Date Notarized	Time ᴬᴹ ᴾᴹ	Fee Charged $

Other Details

Name/Type of Document	Document Date	Right Thumb Print (When Applicable)

Known Personally Y / N	ID Type	Issued By	

ID Checked ☐	ID #	Exp. Date	

Notary Service Performed at:

Witness Name/Address:	Witness Signature:	

| | | Record No. |

Notes/Comments:

Printed Name of Signer	Signer's Signature	Phone No.

Signer's Address

Notary Service(s) Performed ☐ Jurat ☐ Acknowledgment ☐ Oath	Date Notarized	Time ᴬᴹ ᴾᴹ	Fee Charged $

Other Details

Name/Type of Document	Document Date	Right Thumb Print (When Applicable)

Known Personally Y / N	ID Type	Issued By	

ID Checked ☐	ID #	Exp. Date	

Notary Service Performed at:

Witness Name/Address:	Witness Signature:	

| | | Record No. |

Notes/Comments:

Printed Name of Signer	Signer's Signature	Phone No.

Signer's Address

Notary Service(s) Performed ☐ Jurat ☐ Acknowledgment ☐ Oath	Date Notarized	Time AM PM	Fee Charged $

Other Details

Name/Type of Document	Document Date	Right Thumb Print (When Applicable)

Known Personally Y / N	ID Type	Issued By

ID Checked ☐	ID #	Exp. Date

Notary Service Performed at:

Witness Name/Address:	Witness Signature:

Record No.

Notes/Comments:

Printed Name of Signer	Signer's Signature	Phone No.

Signer's Address

Notary Service(s) Performed ☐ Jurat ☐ Acknowledgment ☐ Oath	Date Notarized	Time AM PM	Fee Charged $

Other Details

Name/Type of Document	Document Date	Right Thumb Print (When Applicable)

Known Personally Y / N	ID Type	Issued By

ID Checked ☐	ID #	Exp. Date

Notary Service Performed at:

Witness Name/Address:	Witness Signature:

Record No.

Notes/Comments:

Printed Name of Signer	Signer's Signature	Phone No.

Signer's Address

Notary Service(s) Performed ☐ Jurat ☐ Acknowledgment ☐ Oath	Date Notarized	Time AM PM	Fee Charged $

Other Details

Name/Type of Document	Document Date	Right Thumb Print (When Applicable)
Known Personally Y / N ID Type	Issued By	
ID Checked ☐ ID #	Exp. Date	

Notary Service Performed at:

Witness Name/Address:	Witness Signature:	
		Record No.

Notes/Comments:

Printed Name of Signer	Signer's Signature	Phone No.

Signer's Address

Notary Service(s) Performed ☐ Jurat ☐ Acknowledgment ☐ Oath	Date Notarized	Time AM PM	Fee Charged $

Other Details

Name/Type of Document	Document Date	Right Thumb Print (When Applicable)
Known Personally Y / N ID Type	Issued By	
ID Checked ☐ ID #	Exp. Date	

Notary Service Performed at:

Witness Name/Address:	Witness Signature:	
		Record No.

Notes/Comments:

Printed Name of Signer	Signer's Signature	Phone No.

Signer's Address

Notary Service(s) Performed ☐ Jurat ☐ Acknowledgment ☐ Oath	Date Notarized	Time AM PM	Fee Charged $

Other Details

Name/Type of Document	Document Date	Right Thumb Print *(When Applicable)*

Known Personally Y / N	ID Type	Issued By

ID Checked ☐	ID #	Exp. Date

Notary Service Performed at:

Witness Name/Address:	Witness Signature:

Record No.

Notes/Comments:

Printed Name of Signer	Signer's Signature	Phone No.

Signer's Address

Notary Service(s) Performed ☐ Jurat ☐ Acknowledgment ☐ Oath	Date Notarized	Time AM PM	Fee Charged $

Other Details

Name/Type of Document	Document Date	Right Thumb Print *(When Applicable)*

Known Personally Y / N	ID Type	Issued By

ID Checked ☐	ID #	Exp. Date

Notary Service Performed at:

Witness Name/Address:	Witness Signature:

Record No.

Notes/Comments:

Printed Name of Signer	Signer's Signature	Phone No.

Signer's Address

Notary Service(s) Performed ☐ Jurat ☐ Acknowledgment ☐ Oath	Date Notarized	Time AM PM	Fee Charged $

Other Details

Name/Type of Document	Document Date	Right Thumb Print (When Applicable)

Known Personally Y / N	ID Type	Issued By

ID Checked ☐	ID #	Exp. Date

Notary Service Performed at:

Witness Name/Address:	Witness Signature:

Record No.

Notes/Comments:

Printed Name of Signer	Signer's Signature	Phone No.

Signer's Address

Notary Service(s) Performed ☐ Jurat ☐ Acknowledgment ☐ Oath	Date Notarized	Time AM PM	Fee Charged $

Other Details

Name/Type of Document	Document Date	Right Thumb Print (When Applicable)

Known Personally Y / N	ID Type	Issued By

ID Checked ☐	ID #	Exp. Date

Notary Service Performed at:

Witness Name/Address:	Witness Signature:

Record No.

Notes/Comments:

Made in the USA
Columbia, SC
13 June 2025

59322546R00063